S0-ADI-680

The Bell That Rang for Freedom

BY OLGA W. HALL-QUEST

The Bell That Rang for Freedom

Guardians of Liberty: Sam Adams and John Hancock

How the Pilgrims Came to Plymouth

Jamestown Adventure

Shrine of Liberty: The Alamo

With Stanley in Africa

The Bell That Rang for Freedom

THE LIBERTY BELL AND ITS PLACE IN AMERICAN HISTORY

by Olga W. Hall-Quest

Illustrated by CHRISTINE PRICE

NEW YORK *E. P. Dutton & Co., Inc.*

FIRST EDITION

Published simultaneously in Canada by
Clarke, Irwin & Company Limited, Toronto and Vancouver

Library of Congress Catalog Card Number: 65-21280

PROCLAIM LIBERTY THROUGHOUT ALL THE LAND
UNTO ALL THE INHABITANTS THEREOF. LEV. XXV. 10

Contents

I

Philadelphia, City of the Bell

PHILADELPHIA, the City of Brotherly Love, was founded almost three hundred years ago by the Quakers. From its beginnings, the city that was planted, and that flourished, between two rivers has been a symbol of liberty. Its founder was a great Quaker who granted liberty of conscience to all men. This liberty was the keystone of the code of laws that William Penn framed for the Province of Pennsylvania and the City of Philadelphia. He envisioned the new colony as a haven where people would have the right to worship God in their own way, and where, free from persecution and protected by just laws, they would be happy. He called it the "Holy Experiment."

In England, William Penn had seen the Quakers and other nonconformists hounded and tortured. He had seen them in stocks, jeered and spat upon, and pelted with missiles. He had seen them thrown into prison, under the Quaker Act that made it unlawful for five or more Quakers to gather "under pretense of worship."

George Fox had founded the Society of Friends, and the new religion had spread. Because the Friends warned that men and women should quake, or tremble, in fear of being punished by God, they were also called Quakers.

Since they believed men had the right to serve God without the aid of any priest or minister, the Quakers observed a simple form of worship, and refused to follow the practices of the Established Church of England. Because they thought submission was due to God alone, they would not doff their hats to anyone, not even to the King. Believing all men to be equal in God's sight, they recognized no rank.

William Penn was drawn early to the beliefs and practices of the Friends, and when he was little more than twenty years old he joined them and became a Quaker agitator and defender. His father,

Sir William Penn, who was an admiral in the King's navy, was shocked. To him, his son's use of "thee" and "thou," and his talk about the "inner light," were utter nonsense—and his refusal to lift his hat to his own father and the King an unpardonable insult.

But the Admiral's hopes for a brilliant career for his son in the service of Charles II came to nothing. He lived to hear of the bold and angry eloquence with which young William spoke in defense of the Quakers. Embittered at first, he finally relented and paid fines again and again to secure the young man's release from jail. And in the end, Sir William forgave his son, understood him at last, and left him a large inheritance.

Part of that legacy was an unpaid loan of £16,000 that the Admiral had made to the King. William Penn began to think about how he could use it. Along with other Quakers, he had experienced persecution, and imprisonment in the Tower of London and in the infamous prison of Newgate, and he had been sickened by the misery and the squalor he saw in London.

Dreaming of a fair land where all men would be like brothers, Penn had the practical idea of asking the King for a grant of New World land in payment of his debt. The dream was realized in 1681 when Charles II gave him a charter that made him governor and proprietor of a large tract in America.

The newly appointed Governor suggested the name Sylvania for it, and the King prefixed Penn. Thus the province became Pennsylvania, meaning Penn's Woods.

Early in the year of 1682, Penn sent his cousin William Markham to Pennsylvania to choose a site for a "fair city." He was also instructed to assure the Germans, the Swedes, and the English who had already settled along the Delaware River that their rights would be respected. The location Markham chose lay between two rivers—the broad and beautiful Delaware rolling down to the sea on the east, and, just two miles to the west, the placid Schuylkill winding through primeval forests down to the southeastern point where it emptied into the larger river.

Soon after Markham's return to London, Thomas Holme, the surveyor, sailed for Pennsylvania with William Penn's plan to guide him in laying out the town, which had been named Philadelphia—the City of Brotherly Love.

After land had been cleared by the settlers who came with him, Holme laid out the town in the form of a rectangle, with straight tree-lined streets running from east to west, and from north to south. High Street (now Market) ran from river to river, and Broad Street bisected it halfway between the rivers. At the intersection of these two streets was a center square, and around it, some blocks distant, were four smaller squares that were to be used for city parks. Most of the streets that ran from east to west parallel to High were given the names of trees —Pine, Spruce, Locust, Walnut, Chestnut, and Sassafras. And most of the north-to-south streets parallel to Broad were numbered.

More than anything else, Penn wanted his city to be open and uncrowded, a place where the people could breathe clean air and enjoy the fruits of their own labor and the beauty of their natural surroundings. "Let every house be placed in the middle of its plot," he urged, "so there may be ground on each side for gardens or orchards or fields, that it may be a green country town."

The leaves of the magnificent trees in and around Philadelphia were turning to autumn colors when William Penn came for the first time to his "fair city." His ship *Welcome,* which had sailed from Deal, England, on September 1, 1682, docked at New Castle on October 28. Founded years earlier by the Swedes, New Castle was thirty miles south of Philadelphia, and at this time the only port of any size on the Delaware River. "A glorious river," Penn had said as he sailed up the Delaware for the first time.

It was a young William Penn, thirty-eight years old and tall, handsome, and athletic, who stepped off the *Welcome* that October day—not the pudgy, corpulent old man that the Quaker artist Benjamin West depicted in his famous painting "Penn's Treaty with the Indians." And it is unlikely that he came attired in the somber garb and the broadbrimmed hat that the typical Quaker wore. He was an English gentleman who was fond of dress and comfort, and who was very particular about his hats and flowing wigs. Someone who knew him well wrote that he was "the humblest and liveliest of gentlemen, affable and friendly with the humblest."

Soon after disembarking at New Castle, Penn and a party of friends rowed up the river in an open boat to a landing place where Dock Creek, winding down from Third Street in the heart of Philadelphia, flowed into the Delaware River. They walked across a low, sandy beach to the Blue Anchor Tavern, which stood nearby in a clearing surrounded by stands of pine, walnut, and sycamore trees. Known as a landing house, the tavern operated a ferry that carried people over to Windmill Island, where there was a windmill for grinding grain, and all the way across the river to the Jersey shore. In the vicinity of the Blue Anchor, the small Swedish settlements of Wicaco and Tacony had been founded.

Penn's own people who had preceded him to Philadelphia were at the tavern to greet him that day, and a motley crowd of artisans and laborers, and Swedes and Germans from their tiny settlements. And looking on silently from their canoes were the Indians who had paddled down the creek, flecked with bright leaves, to see the new White

Father, and to wonder how he would treat them.

They need not have worried, for in his relations with the Indians William Penn set an example of fair and considerate treatment that was rarely found elsewhere. When the Treaty of Friendship was drawn up, he said to them: "We meet on the broad pathway of good faith and good will. No advantage shall be taken on either side, but all shall be openness and love."

The Indians came to hold Penn in the highest esteem and affection. They made him a wampum belt of white and purple shells with a design showing a red man and a white man clasping hands. It was given to the great White Sachem as a token of their love and friendship, which would last, the Indians said, "as long as the sun and the moon shall endure."

According to tradition, the wampum belt commemorated the Great Elm Treaty that was negotiated on the river front in Philadelphia near a street named Shackamaxon. The wampum belt has been preserved, but since no written record of the treaty was found, historians do not accept the story as authentic. Whether legend or fact, it truly represents Penn's dealings with the Indians and the enduring bond of friendship between them.

From the beginning, William Penn's "Holy Experiment" was a success. Men who craved the liberty denied them in the old European countries heard of the tolerance practiced by the Quakers and began to emigrate to Pennsylvania. To Philadelphia came craftsmen of all kinds—skilled, honest, humble folk—and artists, scientists, doctors, teachers, ministers, and merchants who would lay the foundation for the city's wealth. And members of every persecuted creed flocked there—Protestants, Catholics, Jews, Moravians, Mennonites, and Dunkards. Penn welcomed them, saying: "I dare not deny others what I crave for myself—liberty for the exercise of my religion."

In 1683, when Penn had served the province for a year as its first governor, he could report that Philadelphia had a ropewalk, a large quay just above Walnut Street, and many "brickeries"—and that brick houses were going up. With abundant and varied building materials at hand, the people showed from the beginning a preference for brick for the construction of their houses and public buildings.

William Penn saw his dream of "a green country town" realized as the little red brick houses went up along the streets of Philadelphia, surrounded by gardens and shaded by fine old trees. Typically, they were two-story houses only two rooms deep, with white trim and white-shuttered windows, and a dormer window extending from a sloping roof. The door might be flush with the street, but more often two or three stone steps led up to the entrance.

But the river front would never be graced by the tree-lined promenade that the founder of the city had planned. Merchants and shipbuilders were quick to see and to exploit the commercial advantages of the "glorious river." There was no Delaware Avenue then. Water Street stretched north and south along the river front, west of it was Front, and beyond that was Second Street.

When the first colonists came to Philadelphia, trees extended down almost to the river along its high banks, from the Blue Anchor landing north to the landing at the Penny-Pot House at Front and Vine streets. The two-story brick house derived its name from an inn that had stood on this site and was known for its beer at a penny a pot. Later it was given another picturesque name, the Jolly Tar Inn, but now a swinging sign advertised its services as the Penny-Pot Free Landing.

Shipyards were soon opened in the same area, and from a second-floor window of the Penny-Pot House a man could swing down to the street below on one of the long jib booms that thrust upward almost to the eaves. There were sawpits, lumberyards, and sail lofts, too, and the wild whortleberry bushes were cleaned out on the site where the first of the ropewalks was built.

After having resided in Philadelphia for two years, William Penn returned to England in 1684. Then, in 1699, he came back for another two years of residence in the Quaker City. During his absence, many property owners had cut narrow lanes and alleys between the streets, and on Penn's second and last visit, he and his family occupied as their winter residence the Slate Roof House at the south-east corner of Norris's Alley and Second Street. Known by its slate roof, it was a large house set in a spacious yard well above street level, and was approached through a double row of tall pines.

Meanwhile, Penn's "fair mansion house" had been completed, and here, at the first sign of spring, he took up residence with his family. Pennsbury Manor was a handsome country estate on the Delaware River a few miles above Philadelphia. The large two-story brick house, with small dormer windows in the mansard roof and a chimney at each end, was elegantly furnished, and the Proprietor and Governor of Pennsylvania entertained here in elegant style. He traveled to and from the city in state, either over the bumpy roads in a coach drawn by four horses, or down the smooth waters of the river in a barge manned by eight oarsmen.

The Governor's barge would tie up at one of the many wharves that jutted out from Water Street all along the river front. White-sailed ships from distant lands berthed alongside the town, and tall cranes lifted their cargoes onto the docks. There they were loaded on wagons and drays that carried them into the city, or to the many warehouses and stores along Front and Water streets. For many years the great and rich merchants of the city lived on these streets in large houses that were both stores and dwelling places.

From the beginning, Philadelphia's merchants had shown a keen business sense in developing the harbor and water-borne trade. Many of them were both shipping merchants and shipowners, and they dealt in a bewildering variety of imports and exports. Immense wealth came to be tied up in vessels and their cargoes. There was, for example, an early merchant who owned twenty ships—square-riggers, brigantines, schooners, and sloops. They brought in rum and sugar from Barbados, linen from Liverpool, rice from South Carolina, tobacco from Virginia, and wine from Madeira. And wheat, flour, iron, furs, lumber, deerskins, bricks, and lime were some of the numerous exports that were shipped to other colonies and abroad.

There were also merchants who added tanneries to their other enterprises. Since the forests of Pennsylvania abounded in wild animals—elk, deer, beavers, raccoons, bears, and foxes—the tanning of hides was an early industry in Philadelphia. William Penn himself had opened a tannery in 1683. The waters of beautiful Dock Creek became so polluted with the wastes from the tanneries located along its banks that in 1784 the creek was filled in and became Dock Street.

Philadelphia's main street took its first name from the incline that sloped down to the river. And the markets that became its characteristic feature for many years gave it the present name of Market. High Street terminated at the river's edge in a wharf and a fish market, and at Second Street in the center of High stood the Town Hall, a quaint structure, tall and narrow, with dormer windows in its steep roof. Just in front of it across Second was a small prison, and directly back of it were the pillory, the stocks, and a whipping post.

The first covered market stalls were set up in the center of High between Front and Second, then between Second and Third, and before they were banished as unsightly obstructions, which was well into the nineteenth century, as far west as Sixth Street. Wednesday and Saturday were market days when the Dutch and the Swedes and farmers from Jersey, across the river, brought produce of all kinds to sell. Here the ladies of Philadelphia came in flower-sprigged muslins and chintzes to do their marketing. A gentleman wrote that he "had no small satisfaction in seeing the pretty creatures traversing the place from stall to stall, some with their maids behind them holding baskets to carry home their purchases."

The area of small shops and retail stores was mainly along Second Street from Arch south to Chestnut, and there were a few on Third, but none could be found on Fourth or Fifth. The city's booksellers and printers had their shops on lower High Street. Here Philadelphia's most distinguished citizen, Benjamin Franklin, opened his first printing shop, and soon added a stationery and bookstore. Later he bought and published the Pennsylvania *Gazette,* which was for many years one of the best of the early American newspapers. Some of the town's famous old inns were located on High Street, too, and between Fourth and Seventh streets, some handsome town houses.

These large houses were built gradually as the wealth of the city increased. Many stood near the small, modest dwellings. Outwardly, they differed only in size and detail. The stately red brick mansions were usually three stories high, with white-shuttered windows and dormer windows projecting from narrow gabled roofs, and were entered through fine white colonial doorways.

It became the custom for wealthy citizens to build country seats, many of them along the lovely Schuylkill, and some fronting upon the Delaware. Such elegant mansions could be seen in no other colony except Virginia. Belmont, Mount Pleasant, Fairhill, Lansdowne, Stenton—these were the names of some of the beautiful country houses that stood in spacious, wooded grounds overlooking one or the other of the two rivers.

By 1748, coaches, wagons, and drays were rattling over cobblestone streets, and property owners were required to sweep the brick-paved sidewalks in front of their shops and houses. But paving came slowly to the Quaker City, and many years passed before there were no more complaints about "the disgrace of suffering the streets to remain long unpaved." Visitors to the city remarked upon the hitching posts spaced along the foot pavements, and the long-handled iron pumps that supplied households with water.

There were nightwatchmen who paced the streets all night, going "round ye town with a small bell" to give notice of the hour and the state of the weather and to rouse the people in an emergency. On October 3, 1751, the *Gazette* announced that "on Monday last the streets began to be illuminated with lamps." And then the lamplighter, shouldering his ladder, became a familiar figure on the streets of the city at dusk.

From the earliest years, taverns, coffeehouses, and inns played an important part in the life of the town, for here men of all classes gathered to relax with a mug of beer, and to discuss business and politics—in the Old London Coffee House at the southwest corner of Front and High streets, in the Pewter Platter Inn between Front and Second streets, and at the Royal Standard Tavern on High Street near Second. It was a man's world pervaded by the pungent aroma of tobacco, ale, and rum.

Sailors, river pilots, ropemakers, caulkers, and shipwrights gathered at the Crooked Billet and Tun Tavern on Water Street for beer and talk of ships and the sea. And in almost every street there was a little pothouse with its swinging signboard where workingmen came for a mug or a pot of beer. One had painted on its board a tree, a bird, a ship, and a mug of beer, and below, this engaging little jingle that must have delighted the customers:

> This is the tree that never grew,
> This is the bird that never flew,
> This is the ship that never sailed,
> This is the mug that never failed.

The men who passed sociable hours at taverns and pothouses on weekdays could be seen in church with their families on Sunday. It would have pleased William Penn if he could have known, years after he died in 1718, that his fair city had become a city of churches in which many faiths were represented.

But Philadelphia's oldest church was standing when the founder was there on his last visit. In the little Swedish settlement of Wicaco, which became part of South Philadelphia, the Swedes had built a small log church in 1677. Then, in 1700, they dedicated a new church on the same site. It was so beautiful that the newcomers called it the "cathedral in the forest." Gloria Dei, which came to be known as the Old Swedes' Church, stood near the Delaware River, surrounded by groves of walnut, pine, sycamore, and hemlock trees. It was a small red brick structure with white trim and steep gables flanking a white doorway. Rising above the steep peaked gables over the main entrance was a square wooden belfry, and topping that a slender white spire. It was the striking angularity of its façade that gave the little church its unique attractiveness.

The first churches that were built in Philadelphia after its founding were the meetinghouses of the Friends, and several were erected before the end of the seventeenth century. In keeping with Quaker beliefs, their houses of worship were plain, substantial brick buildings, unadorned even by belfries and spires. The Moravians and the Mennonites had their plain meetinghouses, too, but most of the members of these sects, and the Dunkards, settled elsewhere in Pennsylvania.

The most beautiful church in Philadelphia was Christ Church on Second Street, a short distance above High Street. Begun in 1727, it was completed in 1754 when its tower and spire were added. On the east façade of the red brick edifice was a large Palladian window, and along its length on both sides were double rows of arched windows, rich in ornamental detail. A massive brick tower adjoined the western end of the church, and above it rose the white wooden belfry and tall spire. The ring of eight bells was cast at the Whitechapel Foundry in London, and was brought over by Captain Richard Budden. He refused to accept payment for this service, and thereafter the bells were rung whenever his ship came up the Delaware.

St. Joseph's, in Willing's Alley near Fourth and Walnut streets, was founded in 1733 when Catholic worship was forbidden everywhere else in colonial America and in Great Britain. St. Peter's, at Third and Pine streets, was another Catholic church; it was completed in 1761. It was notable for its unusually tall brick tower and its soaring white spire. And the early Jewish community worshiped at Mikveh Israel Synagogue up near Sassafras (Race) Street between Third and Fourth. William Penn, the great Quaker liberal, had practiced what he preached—here in his city all men and all creeds had found a home.

In Longfellow's poem *Evangeline* there are memorable lines that evoke the peace and the tolerance of old Philadelphia. It was to Penn's City of Brotherly Love that the poet brought Evangeline at the end of her long wanderings in search of Gabriel—to "that delightful land which is washed by the Delaware's waters":

> There from the troubled sea had Evangeline landed, an exile,
> Finding among the children of Penn a home and a country.

Her ear was pleased by the "thee and thou of the Quakers," and she lived here for many years as a sister of mercy. While visiting the almshouse on a Sunday morning,

> Distant and soft on her ear fell the chimes
> from the belfry of Christ Church,
> While, intermingled with these, across the
> meadows were wafted
> Sounds of psalms, that were sung by the
> Swedes in their church at Wicaco.

And there at the almshouse in Philadelphia, Evangeline found her long-lost lover. But Gabriel died, and in the end the poet left them both peacefully sleeping in the churchyard of St. Joseph's:

> Side by side, in their nameless graves, the
> lovers lie sleeping.
> Under the humble walls of the little Catho-
> lic churchyard,
> In the heart of the city, they lie, unknown
> and unnoticed.

II

Casting the Bell

The Province of Pennsylvania waited a long time for the completion of its State House. Back in 1730, the first lot for its location on the south side of Chestnut Street was purchased on what was to become known as Independence Square many years later. At this time Philadelphia had a population of about 11,500, and was second only to Boston with its 13,000 inhabitants. By 1732, the entire front of Chestnut Street between Fifth and Sixth streets, and extending halfway back to Walnut, had been bought.

It was not until 1769 that the entire square was acquired.

The site that the Assembly chose for the State House was on the southern outskirts of the city. The uneven ground was covered with a rank growth of whortleberry bushes on the north, and there was a peach orchard to the south across Walnut Street.

This location was surveyed by Andrew Hamilton, a brilliant lawyer and at that time Speaker of the Assembly. There were no professional architects in the colonies in those days, but there were cultured men who had enough knowledge of architecture to be able to plan impressive buildings. Andrew Hamilton was one of these gentlemen-architects in Philadelphia, and the Assembly approved his plans for the State House.

Fortunately, the city also had a master carpenter named Edmund Woolley. With nothing more than the rough drawings he himself made of Hamilton's plans, and working under the supervision of the lawyer, he began work on the State House in the early fall of 1732. Ebenezer Tomlinson helped him put up the timbers; John Harrison was the joiner and carver; and Thomas Godfrey did the plastering. Building materials were close at hand—red clay from the riverbanks for the bricks, wood from the forests to the west, a plentiful supply of lime for cement, and marble from nearby quarries.

But work on the building went slowly. This would

be no flimsily constructed edifice, for craftsmen took pride in the quality of their work then, and in Philadelphia there was a scarcity of skilled workmen. Now and again there was a celebration for those who labored on the State House. When the main timbers had been raised, the busy workmen laid down their tools and gathered in the Yard on the south side of the building for a "raising feast." On October 14, 1734, Hannah Powell asked the Assembly for "speedy payment of the balance of my account—for victuals and drink provided for the people employed in the several raisings of the State House." Payment may not have been speedy as Hannah hoped it would be, but in time she had pocketed the considerable sum of £88.19.1, all of it paid out to her by the provincial government.

Three years went by, and in September 1735, the Assembly met for the first time in the eastern chamber on the first floor of the State House. Even then, the walls had not been paneled and some of the windows were without glass panes. But early in the following year the wings of the central building were completed, and provincial officials moved into them. The wings stood a short distance from the east and west walls of the State House, and were connected with it by arcades, or "piazzas," each of which contained a stairway that led to the second floor of the wings and was closed on the south side by a brick wall. Sometimes visiting Indians were lodged in one of the wings, but they were so careless with fire that the nervous Assembly ordered a separate building erected for them in 1759, possibly one of the two wooden sheds that stood for some years at the corners of Fifth and Sixth streets on Chestnut.

Work inside the State House dragged on, with the legislators jogging the workmen, at times losing patience with them, and almost despairing of ever having a finished building. At last, in February 1748, it *was* completed. Fifteen years abuilding was a long time, but the carpenters, the brickmasons, the painters, and the plasterers had done their work not only well but beautifully. The group of red brick buildings, with white doorways and white trim around the window frames, stood as an admirable example of colonial architecture—simple, graceful, and harmonious.

In January 1750, two years after the completion of the State House, the Assembly decided that the building needed a tower with a staircase leading up to a belfry. So Edmund Woolley came back with a crew of workmen and began construction on the new addition against the south side of the State House.

The work was in progress when the legislators met on October 15, 1751, and on that date made another decision—one that proved to be momentous. Speaker Isaac Norris presided at the meeting, and the talk that early fall afternoon was about the urgent need of a good bell for the State House. From the earliest years of the Province, a bell had been used to summon the members of the Assembly together and had been rung for official proclamations and other public functions. Probably the first bell had been brought over by William Penn himself. This bell was hung in the crotch of a tree during the years when the legislators had to meet in private dwellings, in schoolrooms, or in the Quaker meetinghouses.

Now they would have a proper bell, a great bell with a voice that could carry much farther than that of the smaller one, for on that October afternoon the Assembly authorized the superintendents of the State House to order a new bell from the mother country—"a bell of such weight and dimensions as they shall think suitable." Because no large bell had yet been cast in the colonies, the order had to be placed with the foundry in London that had cast the ring of bells for Christ Church.

During the last two weeks in October, the three superintendents—Isaac Norris, Thomas Leech, and Edward Warner—worked on plans for the bell. Like his father before him, Isaac Norris was a wealthy Quaker who served the Province of Pennsylvania long and faithfully. He was a scholarly man with a sound knowledge of Hebrew and Latin, and while the superintendents were searching for a suitable inscription for the bell, it was quite likely he who turned to the Bible and singled out Leviticus 25:10.

In this passage, the people of Israel were instructed to hold a jubilee every fifty years in commemoration of their liberation from Egypt. It begins: "And ye shall hallow the fiftieth year, and proclaim liberty throughout all the land unto all the inhabitants thereof."

Quite likely, too, it seemed an appropriate inscription for the bell because in that year of 1751 the colonists were celebrating the fiftieth anniversary of William Penn's great Charter of Privileges to the Province of Pennsylvania. Issued in 1701, it granted full religious freedom to the people of the Province, a measure of personal liberty that none of the other colonists had.

The words of the inscription that came to be cast on the bell were not related to American independence, as is often assumed, for independence would not come until twenty-five years later. But it was as if Isaac Norris and his associates had had prophetic vision—as if they had been able to look far into the future and see the day when their bell would proclaim the liberty that came with the Declaration of Independence in 1776.

By November 1, 1751, they had drafted the letter that was sent under that date to Robert Charles, the colonial agent of the Province in London. Addressed as "Respected Friend," he was asked to procure "a good bell of about 2,000 pounds weight."

"We hope and rely on thy care and assistance in

this affair," the superintendents wrote further, "and that thou wilt procure and forward it by the first good opportunity, as our workmen inform us it will be much less trouble to hang the bell before their scaffolds are struck from the building where we intend to place it, which will not be done till the end of next summer or beginning of the fall."

It was urged that the bell be cast by the best founders, and with the following words "well-shaped in large letters" around its crown:

> PROCLAIM LIBERTY THROUGHOUT ALL THE LAND UNTO ALL THE INHABITANTS THEREOF. LEV. XXV. 10

And beneath the inscription:

> By order of the Assembly of the Province of Pennsylvania for the State House in the City of Philadelphia, 1752.

While the tower went up brick by brick, and Edmund Woolley supervised its construction, the founders at Thomas Lester's Whitechapel Foundry in London labored over the great bell that the Assembly's superintendents had ordered. Perhaps Friend Robert Charles, the colonial agent, came now and again to check on the progress of the work, for Isaac Norris did not let him forget the Assembly's concern for the bell. Some weeks before it came, he wrote: "We are looking for the bell daily." Friend Charles must have visualized the anxious legislators standing beside the Delaware, gazing downriver in the hope of seeing Captain Budden's ship coming with their treasure.

And the day did come in that August of 1752 when a stout ship sailed up the broad river with the bell on board. Captain Budden had brought it safely across the ocean, and it was safely deposited on a Philadelphia dock.

The brick tower was not finished, and there was no belfry yet, but the bell was set up in the State House Yard for testing. To everyone's disappointment and to the mortification of Speaker Norris, "the bell was cracked by a stroke of the clapper without any other violence." The superintendents quickly concluded that it should be sent back at once to the Whitechapel Foundry. But Captain Budden already had a full cargo for the return voyage, and there was no room on his ship for the bell.

In this distressful situation two humble ironworkers came forward and offered to recast the bell at their iron foundry. John Pass and Charles Stow had never cast a bell before, but they were "ingenious workmen" who were willing to try. It seemed to them, and to others who judged the calamitous cracking of the bell, that Thomas Lester's founders had done something that made it "too high and brittle." It was decided that a mixture of an ounce and a half of copper to a pound of the bell metal was what it needed. Pass and Stow broke up the bell, melted it down, and poured the molten metal into what Isaac Norris described as a "masterly mould."

Since the novices at bell casting did not discourage visitors to the foundry, the assemblymen came to watch their bell being recast. The brawny founders, with gray shirt sleeves rolled up and knee breeches covered by big leather aprons, handled the hot tools and the molten metal expertly. The gentlemen—some wearing tricornered hats and bright-hued coats, and the Quakers in sober gray and broadbrimmed headgear—stood around the blazing furnace, and gaped.

Superintendent Norris had seen that the metal "ran well" into the "masterly mould," and everyone watched with pride and excitement when the recast bell was lifted onto a wagon and brought back to the State House Yard. Here it was again hung up on trusses for testing, and again the huge clapper struck the sides of the bell resoundingly. No crack appeared this time, but the jangling tone did not bring applause for the hopeful founders. Instead, there was laughter, and Pass and Stow were "so teased by the witticisms of the town" that they were stung into making another attempt at casting a good bell.

On the second trial they succeeded. The bell had a strange sound, unlike that of any bell the people had ever heard, but they had nothing but praise this time for Pass and Stow. Isaac Norris was elated. "This is probably the earliest casting of a large bell in English America," he declared. And it was the Assembly of the Province of Pennsylvania that "first ventured upon and succeeded in the greatest bell" cast in the American colonies. The Speaker would have been even more puffed with pride if he could have known in that spring of 1753 how famous the Bell would become.

Not since work had begun on the State House had there been such a raising feast as was given in honor of the Bell, and of Pass and Stow. Tables were set up in the Yard and loaded with food—with huge quantities of beef, cheese, potatoes, bread, and three gallons of rum punch and a barrel of beer. Edmund Woolley's men did no more work that day. With candles on hand, the celebration continued into the evening.

In June of 1753, the four-story brick tower was completed. Centered against the south side of the State House, with a wooden belfry and a steeple on top, the tower greatly enhanced the beauty of the building. A handsome Palladian window above the white doors, and other architectural details, added charm and interest to the structure. After the addition of clock faces in the end walls just below the eaves, no other changes were made during the colonial period. Here, then, was the State House, with its graceful lines and pleasing proportions, with its dignity and restraint, that became the birthplace of the nation.

And at last the 2,080-pound Bell was hoisted up into the belfry. If it had not cracked when it was first tested, the name of the Whitechapel Foundry would have appeared on it. Instead, it bore the simple names of Pass and Stow, and the Bell immortalized the two humble founders. For a very long time, though, no one gave much thought to the noble inscription that encircled the crown of the Bell:

PROCLAIM LIBERTY THROUGHOUT ALL THE LAND UNTO ALL THE INHABITANTS THEREOF. LEV. XXV. 10.

III

Taxation Without Representation

In the afternoon of August 27, 1753, Philadelphia's citizens were startled by such a clangor as they had not heard before. Shopkeepers and housewives paused to listen to the penetrating clang. This was no familiar ding-dong, and when the last reverberations had died away, more than one citizen could have been heard to say, "It's that outlandish Bell at the State House."

They were right. It was the first summons by the Bell to the assemblymen to gather for a meeting in their chamber at the State House. The spirit of independence was evident at the meeting on that August afternoon. The legislators resolved "to make and continue the issue of the Province's money, notwithstanding the order of the Lords Justices of the Crown." They argued that the Assembly had the right under the Charter of the Province to enact any laws whatsoever for raising money for the public use.

Perhaps Pennsylvania's Assembly could flout the order of the Lords Justices because England was preoccupied at this time with the last phase of her long-drawn-out struggle with France for possession of the American colonies. There had been fighting in the Ohio Valley along Pennsylvania's western border, but the war had by-passed Philadelphia. England was not helped in this war by the full cooperation of her colonies. Each colony was inclined to ignore the mother country's pleas for money and troops unless threatened itself by the French. Little assistance came from Pennsylvania, one of the most prosperous and populous of the colonies, and vitally situated.

The Quakers were in control in the eastern part of the Province, and since they would not take up arms even in self-defense, they contributed little to the war effort. The German and Scotch-Irish colonists in western Pennsylvania bore most of the burden. The Friends in Philadelphia went on supporting their almshouse and numerous other charities—and asserting their independence, confident that their way of governing Philadelphia was the right way.

On May 17, 1755, the Bell called the legislators to another spirited session in which they sharply reminded the Governor of their "rights as Englishmen." Were they in a position in which they had to enact laws dictated to them? Quite indignantly, they informed the Governor that they did not desire independence that was not authorized by the Constitution, but—and here they made their point—"The Constitution gives us the right to judge for ourselves what laws are just and proper for our people."

The Assembly was also involved in a quarrel with William Penn's sons, Thomas and Richard, who were now the proprietors of the colony. Unlike their father, the sons had little concern for the welfare of the colonists. They lived in London and were interested in the Province of Pennsylvania only as a source of income. The Assembly finally demanded the right to tax their colonial property.

On the third of February 1757, the Bell pealed for the meeting at which the assemblymen decided they would have to send "Mr. Franklin home to England" to smooth out their differences with Penn's heirs. Mr. Franklin was not a Quaker, but this remarkable man was highly esteemed by Friends and non-Quakers alike, and he had, moreover, already earned an international reputation.

He was Benjamin Franklin who, at the age of seventeen, had run away from his home in Boston and had arrived in Philadelphia on a Sunday morning in October 1723. He had come to a strange city with little more than the clothes he wore, but he was confident that he could make a living in the printing business.

The boy who had learned the printer's trade from his older brother in Boston rose fast. At twenty-four, he had his own printing shop and was impressing the thrifty Quakers by trundling the paper he bought through the streets in a wheelbarrow. He purchased the run-down Pennsylvania *Gazette* and built it into the foremost newspaper in the colonies.

And when he was twenty-six, Franklin decided to publish a paperbound, pocket-size almanac. He had the inspired idea of filling "all the little spaces that occur between the remarkable days of the calendar with proverbial sentences"—and the "Sayings of Poor Richard" was born. Published expressly for the common people, the sayings of Poor Richard became familiar to people of all classes throughout the colonies and in countries abroad, particularly in France and England.

Benjamin Franklin was himself a shining example of the industry and thrift that he preached in so many of his maxims. He may not habitually have gone to bed and risen early—how could he have accomplished so much if he had?—but he became wealthy and wise. In 1748, when he was just forty-two years old, he was able to retire from business.

In Penn's Quaker City, Franklin found the freedom of thought and the tolerance that were so congenial to his reasonable spirit. Philadelphia became his city, as Boston could never have been, and in the years before and after his retirement from business, he stamped his own image unforgettably upon it. He seems to have had a hand in whatever was useful and beneficial for the town and the Province.

It was Franklin who organized Philadelphia's first fire department, reorganized its police force, and was largely responsible for lighting and paving the streets. He served as a member of the Assembly, was postmaster of the city, and helped to organize and finance the first free hospital in the colonies. His name was on its first board of managers, and on nearly every other board of managers in Philadelphia. When the Quaker assemblymen refused to vote money for the defense of the city, Franklin called mass meetings and single-handedly got militia companies organized and armed. And, in 1753, he became the highly efficient deputy postmaster general of the northern colonies.

Always interested in the spreading of knowledge, Franklin conceived the idea of a public library that would lend its books to subscribers to be carried home "into the bosom of private families." With the help of friends, he formed such a subscription library that was later incorporated as the Library Company of Philadelphia. He also founded the University of Pennsylvania and the American Philosophical Society, which was the first scientific association for the "promotion of useful knowledge."

And in the field of science and invention, Benjamin Franklin was himself endlessly inventive and amazingly active. He invented the lightning rod and made important discoveries about the phenomenon of electricity, though there is no record of his ever having performed the famous kite experiment to prove that lightning and electricity were identical. The legend of Franklin and his kite came to be as indestructible as that of George Washington and the cherry tree. For his solid achievements Harvard and Yale conferred honorary degrees upon him in 1753, and in that decade he became known throughout Europe as America's leading scientist.

Philadelphia also owed its first willow tree to Franklin's keen observation and his alert interest in even the smallest things. One day he happened to notice a willow twig woven into a rough basket that stood on the deck of a boat anchored in the river. He plucked out the fragile shoot and carried it to the young daughter of Isaac Norris. Debby Norris planted and tended it carefully in her father's beautiful gardens at Fairhill, and in time people came to marvel at the "weeping" branches of the first willow tree they had ever seen.

While Benjamin Franklin conferred with Penn's sons about the affairs of the Province, attended meetings of learned groups, and charmed London society with his wit, momentous events occurred.

In 1759, a victory for the British on the Plains of Abraham gave them possession of Quebec. The following year, when Montreal fell to them, the war with France in America was over. And in October of that year of 1760, George II died.

There was a joyous ringing of church bells in Philadelphia on the twenty-first of February 1761, and the clanging of the great Bell brought a vast crowd to the State House Yard to hear George III proclaimed King. After the ceremony, the Bell rang again, and the people shouted, "Long live King George III!"

The new monarch of Great Britain was young, just twenty-two years old when he ascended the throne, and although not handsome, he looked impressively royal in velvet and ermine. As well he might, for he was the ruler of the most powerful country in Europe—of the greatest naval and colonial power in the world now that France had at last been vanquished. But Great Britain had paid dearly for her triumphs on land and sea. Her treasury was drained, and there was a tremendous public debt that had to be paid.

It was an ominous coincidence that in the same month and the same year in which George III was proclaimed King, an angry and eloquent protest against the policies of the mother country was voiced in Boston, Massachusetts.

The old Acts of Trade and the Navigation Acts placed severe restrictions upon colonial trade. But for years enforcement had been lax, and resenting the injustice of the measures, the merchants had taken to smuggling. England tried with but little success to combat the illegal trade with writs of assistance—warrants that gave customs officers the right to search ships and warehouses for contraband goods. When George III came to the throne, customs officers in Boston stepped up the seizure of illicit cargoes with writs that also gave them entry into private dwellings. Furious, the shipping merchants appealed to the Massachusetts Superior Court.

It was James Otis, a brilliant young lawyer, who stood before the crimson-robed judges on a cold February afternoon in 1761 and thundered, "A man is as secure in his house as a prince in his castle." He did not question the legality of the writs, but he warned darkly, "I oppose that kind of power the exercise of which, in former periods of English history, cost one King of England his head and another his throne."

Another and younger lawyer, who at twenty-six was just beginning his legal practice in Massachusetts, heard the impassioned argument and was moved to say, "Otis was a flame of fire. Then and there, the child independence was born." He was John Adams—a short, roly-poly man, bluntly honest, and sharply logical and outspoken.

Otis's appeal in behalf of the merchants of Massachusetts should have given the newly crowned King pause for earnest and searching thought about British policy toward the American colonies. Had he been wise, he would have seen that the American colonials were not a servile people easily coerced into obedience. They had found in the New World the liberty that had been denied them in their homeland. Far removed from the mother country, they had grown self-reliant and independent in spirit. In their colonial legislatures they had learned how to govern themselves and how to manage their own affairs. And now that they were no longer dependent on England for protection against the French, they would be increasingly resentful of strict control.

But George III was not wise. He did not understand the Americans, and he did not have the qualities of statesmanship that were necessary to govern a great empire wisely and well. He was temperate, industrious, and conscientious in his efforts to be a good king, but these personal virtues were not enough. And there were no statesmen among the King's ministers. They, too, lacked wisdom, imagination, and insight into the problems of government.

The immediate problem was how to raise money to defray the expenses of the costly wars that had formally ended with the signing of the Peace of Paris in 1763. Since the people in England were already heavily taxed, the King and his ministers turned to the American colonies for additional revenue. And why not? they reasoned, since the colonies were prosperous, and the French and Indian Wars had been fought for their benefit, too.

So the first fumbling, unwise step was taken in March 1764 when the English Parliament approved the Sugar Act—in America called the Molasses Act. It had been introduced by George Grenville, Chancellor of the Exchequer, and a man singularly lacking in vision but exceptionally good at bookkeeping. His new revenue act raised the tax on sugar and reduced the duty on molasses by half, but strict enforcement would leave no loophole for smuggling from the French and Spanish West Indies. And it was from these non-British islands that New Englanders smuggled most of the molasses they used in the profitable distilling trade—in making rum.

But Sam Adams, Boston's "watchdog of liberty," saw in the Sugar Act a threat to the charter rights of the colonies to govern and tax themselves. Studying the text of the act closely, he read that it was "just and necessary that a revenue be raised for defraying the expenses of defending the colonies."

"If taxes are laid upon us in any shape," he argued, "without our having a legal representation where they are laid, are we not reduced from the character of subjects to the miserable state of tributary slaves?"

This was the first public denial of the right of the British Parliament to tax the colonies without their consent, and it was made by the man who dedicated his life to bringing about an independent America. Sam Adams was not a great orator or a great statesman—he was a shrewd politician who worked tirelessly for the cause of American liberty. He fought so ruthlessly against any infringement of colonial rights that the royal governor of Massachusetts called him the "Chief Incendiary." And Sam Adams called every act of infringement by King George and Parliament a "menacing monster."

Those who were opposed to the royal governors and the British Parliament were known as Whigs, and the defenders of the Crown were called Tories. Canny Sam Adams made a practice of luring bright young men into the Whig camp. One of the brightest was his cousin John Adams, thirteen years younger than Sam. And he had snared the young aristocrat, John Hancock, who was the wealthiest merchant in New England. There was the gifted Paul Revere, too, leader of the large artisan class—carpenters, shipwrights, and other craftsmen—that was solidly behind Sam Adams.

Boston patriots met often at clubs and taverns—at the Green Dragon and the Bunch of Grapes—and in snug, secret garrets to talk about colonial rights and grievances. Young men met in the Raleigh Tavern, too, down in Williamsburg, Virginia, for long and probing discussions about liberty. Virginians were not affected by the Sugar Act, but young Thomas Jefferson and Patrick Henry, particularly, were concerned about the implications of the act that agitated Sam Adams.

It was from the colonies of Massachusetts and Virginia that leadership in the revolutionary movement came. There were no patriots in Pennsylvania who rose to defy the authority of King and Parliament. But the power of the nonresistant Quakers in the Assembly was waning, and other members were caught up in the wave of patriotic fervor that rolled westward from Boston.

Meanwhile, in England, George Grenville had been busy at his bookkeeping. Clearly, more money had to come from the American colonials, not only to help pay off Britain's war debt but also to meet part of the cost of maintaining a standing army in the colonies. It occurred to Grenville that since the people in England had long been used to stamp taxes, why would the colonists object to them? Moreover, the taxes he proposed to levy would fall equally upon all the colonies and upon all classes. So in February 1765, Parliament passed the Stamp Act, which would not go into force until the following November.

No one in Parliament had questioned the wisdom

of the act except Colonel Isaac Barré, and in his defense of the colonists he called them "sons of liberty." His speech was published in America, and soon afterward patriots who rebelled against the injustices of the mother country were known as Sons of Liberty.

There was consternation in America when the people learned that they would have to buy stamps for all commercial papers and documents—for newspapers, wills, deeds, and even for a college diploma, which would cost two pounds. Up to now there had been almost no unity among the thirteen colonies, but with a grievance common to all, they were united for the first time in outraged protest.

Feeling against the Stamp Act became so bitter that violence erupted. In all the colonies there were riots, and many of the stamp collectors, who had been appointed by the Crown, were tarred and feathered by the Sons of Liberty and driven out of town. The hated stamps were seized and burned, or the ships that had brought them were not allowed to come into port. In Boston, a howling mob wound up an evening of vandalism by plundering and wrecking the beautiful home of Lieutenant Governor Thomas Hutchinson.

But there was more than mob violence. Addressing the House of Burgesses in Virginia, Patrick Henry loosed his oratorical lightning in an impassioned speech in which he boldly warned George III to profit from the example of Caesar who had his Brutus, and Charles the First his Cromwell. And the historic Stamp Act Congress was held in New York in October 1765. Twenty-eight representatives from nine colonies came together to discuss the act, and to protest in resolves and a petition to Parliament that taxation without representation was tyranny.

Then the merchants in Boston and other colonial towns cut off British trade with a boycott so effective that indignant businessmen and manufacturers in England bombarded Parliament with protests against the Stamp Act. Benjamin Franklin was back in London after a brief visit to Philadelphia, and as agent for Pennsylvania he warned that if British soldiers were sent to America to enforce the act, they would not find a rebellion but they might make one. The British government had to admit defeat, and in March 1766, the Stamp Act was repealed.

When the news of repeal reached the colonies, there was unrestrained joy and celebration in all the towns. On May 20, 1766, the brig *Minerva* brought the happy tidings to Philadelphia, and the Bell in the State House steeple rang and rang, accompanied by the silvery chiming of the church bells. Kegs of beer were rolled into the streets for the poor, the Mayor presided over a sumptuous banquet in the long room at the State House, and bonfires blazed all night.

The peace and calm that followed were short-lived. Almost no one except Sam Adams had given thought to the threat in the Declaratory Act that was passed along with the Stamp Act. It asserted that Parliament had the right to make laws governing the colonies "in all cases whatsoever." And the colonists believed just as strongly that they had the right to tax themselves—that there should be no taxation by Parliament without representation. By fearlessly flouting the Stamp Act, they had shown that they would fight for a principle, too.

But George III did not heed the warnings, and his ministers and Parliament blundered on, never doubting the wisdom of their measures or Great Britain's authority over her colonies.

In 1767, the Townshend Acts followed the Stamp Act. Now taxes were levied on paint, glass, lead, paper, and tea. Sam Adams cried "Tyranny!" seized his quill pen, and drafted a circular letter of protest that the other colonies applauded. But a stinging rebuke came from England in June 1768 from Lord Hillsborough, Colonial Secretary of State. Outrageous, he declared, and "calculated to inflame the minds of good subjects."

Boston ignored the order to rescind the "inflammatory" letter, and Sam Adams's Mohawks, as the Tories called the town's Sons of Liberty, began terrorizing the customs commissioners. The royal Governor appealed to the mother country "to rescue the Government from the hands of a trained mob."

The response to this plea was the quartering of British troops in the town to act as a police force. The arrival of the redcoats was an intolerable insult to the people, and there were the inevitable clashes that culminated in the Boston Massacre. The troops had been taunted beyond endurance, and although only five Bostonians were killed in the encounter between the redcoats and a mob on the night of March 5, 1770, Sam Adams's propaganda blew up the incident into the "horrid massacre." It was serious enough, however, for the liberty-loving colonists were being goaded into armed rebellion, as Benjamin Franklin had predicted they might be.

On the day of the "massacre" the Townshend Acts were repealed—all the duties except that on tea. There had been another boycott of English goods, and such formidable protests that the acts could not be enforced. But the British government stubbornly retained the tax on tea to show its authority.

And tea led to the most disastrous blunder of all on the part of King, Cabinet, and Parliament. Having a monopoly of the English tea business, the East India Company had found a lucrative market in America where tea was the favorite beverage of the colonists. When mismanagement brought the company close to bankruptcy, it raised the price of its tea. There was a sharp drop in the amount it exported to the colonies when colonial merchants began smuggling tea from the Dutch East Indies.

With extreme lack of wisdom, the Prime Minister, Lord North, undertook to help the East India Company out of its financial difficulties by trying to force the tea-drinking Americans into buying its huge surplus stored in warehouses in London. In May 1773, Parliament passed the Tea Act, which gave the Company a monopoly in the American market. The tax would be slight—the tea would actually cost less than that the colonists smuggled from the Dutch East Indies. But Company-appointed consignees would sell it, not the colonial merchants, who would thus be cut out.

When news of Parliament's arrangements to sell the East India Company's tea reached America, indignation blazed from Maine to Georgia. In Philadelphia, the Bell rang furiously, and crowds gathered in the State House Yard to cheer the Assembly's resolutions denouncing the Tea Act as a violent attack upon American liberties. The Bell rang again, and triumphantly, when the largest throng ever to assemble in the Yard hailed the resolve not to permit Captain Ayres to unload the *Polly*'s cargo of tea on the city's wharves. And "the ship, the captain, and the tea sailed down the river to return no more."

At other ports the same procedure took place—the ships were forced to swing around and take the detested tea back to England. And in all the towns, the Sons of Liberty harassed the consignees.

Riotous Boston climaxed the opposition by staging its celebrated Tea Party. More than a hundred "Indians," armed with "tomahawks" and axes, whooped down to Griffin's Wharf on the moonlit night of December 16, 1773, and boarded the three tea ships. Before dawn, 342 chests of the finest English bohea had been dumped into the harbor. The incoming tide washed tea along the beaches in great drifts all the way from Boston to Dorchester. There had been no interference by the British troops, who had been removed after the "massacre" to the fort on Castle Island at the entrance to the harbor.

But this time George III did not yield. Boston had provoked the King's wrath, and Boston would be punished. The Boston fanatics would be taught that they could not flout the laws of His Majesty's government with impunity. It would be a lesson and a warning to all the American colonies.

News of the punitive measures came on May 10, 1774—news of the Coercive Acts. On the first of June the port of Boston was to be closed and blockaded by British warships until the town agreed to pay for the tea that had been destroyed. Thereafter, Salem was to be the capital of Massachusetts. And General Thomas Gage would be the military governor who would be stationed in Boston to maintain order there, and in the colony, with British troops.

Paul Revere carried word of Boston's plight and an appeal for support to New York and Philadelphia. He had already become the leading express rider of the patriots in Boston, for his judgment and reliability could be trusted, and his devotion to the cause of freedom was unquestioned. On this long, hard ride, he also handed out broadsides of the Boston Port Bill along the way.

On the fateful day of June 1, flags on all the ships in the harbor of Philadelphia were lowered to half-mast. Nearly every shop was closed, but the churches were open as if it were Sunday, and the people came to listen to appropriate sermons.

Andrew McNair, doorkeeper of the Assembly and bellringer at the State House, climbed the tower stairs to the belfry, muffled the great Bell, and slowly tolled it. Here in Philadelphia, and elsewhere in the colonies, the first of June 1774 was a funereal day in observance of the closing of the port of Boston.

IV

The Deepening Crisis

AS ANGER boiled up against Great Britain and more meetings were held in the State House Yard, the Bell atop Philadelphia's State House rang with increasing frequency. Finally, "divers inhabitants" living near the State House formally protested the too-frequent ringing of the great Bell. It caused them much distress, they stated, and most severely "when some of the petitioners' families have been affected with sickness, at which times, from the Bell's uncommon size and unusual sound, it is extremely dangerous and may prove fatal."

The assemblymen were more concerned about the condition of the steeple after carpenters examined it and reported that the timbers showed signs of weakening. Though excessive ringing of the Bell was discouraged for that reason, it did continue to ring. It rang on the eighteenth of June 1774 when the people gathered in the Yard to discuss Boston's critical situation. At that meeting they pledged the city "to the common cause of liberty," and contributed generously to the relief of the Boston sufferers.

Messages of sympathy poured into the blockaded town, and carts laden with gifts of food came in over the narrow neck that joined Boston to the mainland. The letter from the Sons of Liberty in Norfolk, Virginia, expressed what all the colonies felt. "Be assured," they wrote, "that we consider you as suffering in the common cause, and look upon ourselves as bound by the most sacred ties to support you."

What Thomas Jefferson felt about the tyrannous measures the British government had taken against Boston, and all previous oppressive acts, was expressed in a pamphlet of twenty-three pages entitled "A Summary View of the Rights of British America." Written in the summer of 1774, it boldly and indignantly denied the right of Parliament to interfere in the internal affairs of the colonies. "The God who gave us life gave us liberty at the same time," Jefferson wrote, speaking not only for Americans, but for all people everywhere.

The colonists were not at a loss to know what to do at this time of grave crisis. Acting through their committees of correspondence, and in their provincial legislatures, they made plans to hold a congress in Philadelphia. John and Sam Adams were the most prominent of the delegates elected to represent Massachusetts, and Sam's friends thoughtfully provided him with a new wardrobe, from wig to buckled shoes. It would not have occurred to him that he would cut a sorry figure in his shiny old brown suit, for he was indifferent to everything except the fight for liberty.

The delegates who came to Philadelphia early in September 1774 for the First Continental Congress were impressed by this largest and richest town in the colonies. They found a society that was "happy, elegant, tranquil, and polite," and so hospitable that the visitors were wined and dined prodigiously. John Adams cheerfully admitted enjoying the "sinful feasts," but Cousin Sam, the austere old Puritan, abhorred luxurious living, and found pleasure in exploring the waterfront, where he chatted with sailors and dockworkers just as he did in Boston.

At ten o'clock on the Monday morning of September 5, the State House Bell and all the church bells of Philadelphia pealed a welcome to the forty-odd delegates who had assembled at the "genteel and elegant" City Tavern. This was a new tavern, located on Second Street near Walnut, where stagecoaches and stage wagons arrived and from which they departed. A few blocks to the west was Carpenters' Hall, which had been chosen as the meeting place of the first Congress. It had just been completed by the Carpenters' Company—a simple two-story brick building with a pedimented façade and a graceful white cupola.

The delegates walked the short distance to the Hall in a body, and after inspecting the building, seated themselves in armchairs in the east room on the first floor, a small bright chamber with a white-paneled fireplace.

Thomas Jefferson was not present at this first Congress, but there were other distinguished Virginians. Peyton Randolph served as President, and Colonel George Washington, a tall, broad-shouldered man, was there. Wearing the blue-and-buff uniform of the Fairfax County militia, he was the only delegate in uniform. Now forty-two years old, he had fought with exceptional bravery in the French and Indian War. Washington had immense dignity and, though he rarely spoke, commanded respect. Virginia was represented, too, by its great orator, Patrick Henry—a slight, plainly dressed man with intense blue eyes deep-set in a long, narrow face—and by Richard Henry Lee, "tall, spare, and a deep thinker."

Nobody except Sam Adams was yet ready to urge independence. There were many who feared his hot-headed radicalism and said he wanted Massachusetts to be the head of America, Boston the head of Massachusetts, and himself dictator of Boston. Aware of this distrust, the delegates from the Bay Province were cautious, but Sam Adams worked hard at what he could do best—behind-the-scenes wirepulling and maneuvering for political advantage.

The Congress drafted a moderate "Declaration of Rights" in which grievances were restated and the Coercive Acts condemned as unconstitutional, and a "Loyal Address to the King" was drawn up. But the decision to come to Boston's aid with an armed force if the British troops should take the offensive was a victory for the Massachusetts men. The Congress also approved arming the local militia, and other defense measures, and adopted the Continental Association—another nonimportation agreement.

At the beginning of the sessions, Patrick Henry had electrified the delegates when he said: "The distinctions between Virginians, Pennsylvanians, New Yorkers, and New Englanders are no more. I am not a Virginian but an American!"

It was yet another warning to stubborn, short-sighted George III. The First Continental Congress adjourned on October 26, and in the following month of November 1774, the King told his minister, Lord North: "The New England governments are in a state of rebellion. Blows must decide whether they are to be subject to this country or independent." It was instead rebellion on a continental scale that was blowing up like a hurricane.

Benjamin Franklin was near despair over the widening chasm between the American colonies and the mother country. For more than a decade, he had served Pennsylvania and other colonies as their colonial agent in London. He had been made a member of the Royal Society and awarded a gold medal. After Saint Andrews and Oxford conferred honorary degrees upon him, this self-taught man was called Dr. Franklin.

As much at home in London as he was in Philadelphia, the utterly reasonable Dr. Franklin had believed a break between Great Britain and her colonies could be avoided, and he had labored patiently to this end. But he had pleaded in vain for justice and fair treatment on the part of the British government, and now Lord North was calling him "the most malicious and dangerous enemy in Great Britain."

King George and his ministers even refused to listen to the counsel of those English statesmen who warned them of the folly of trying to coerce the Americans. In the House of Lords, old William Pitt, now Lord Chatham, declared: "All attempts to impose servitude upon such a mighty continental nation must be in vain." And Edmund Burke, pleading for conciliation, was ignored.

In March 1775, the Virginia Convention was held in Richmond, where the burgesses were free from the control of the royal governor. Here, in Old St. John's Church, Patrick Henry argued that measures should be taken for armed resistance to Great Britain, warning that "the next gale that sweeps from the north will bring the clash of resounding arms." And in this speech he uttered his most famous words: "Give me liberty or give me death!" The "clash of resounding arms" came soon afterward.

General Thomas Gage had been so confident that he could tame rebellious Boston. All that was needed, he had told King George, was "to take the resolute part"—that and four British regiments would soon put out the fires of rebellion.

But Gage's efforts to control the rebel patriots failed. Beyond the range of his guns in Boston, the Massachusetts voters elected a Provincial Congress. Under the leadership of John Hancock, it collected and stored military supplies and supervised the training of militia. Citizens, armed and ready to fight at a minute's notice, came into action as the minutemen. And on every village green they could be seen at their drills, banging away with old squirrel guns and dressed, not in fine uniforms, but in nondescript homespun and leather breeches.

After almost a year of confinement in Boston,

Gage's troops had become bored and restless. Prodded by his officers and criticized by the King, he finally decided to act. He made elaborate preparations for sending out a large force to take the military stores he knew the patriots had hidden in Concord, and hopefully, Sam Adams and John Hancock, who were known to be somewhere near Lexington.

Every move that the British made was observed and reported by the alert Sons of Liberty—by the mechanics who prowled the streets at night, never relaxing their vigilance. And at the center of all the activity to thwart the British was bold Revere. It was he who carried intelligence reports to Dr. Joseph Warren, the only Whig leader in Boston, and from him received orders to act. Together they planned the lantern signals that would inform Colonel William Conant in Charlestown whether the British were marching by land or leaving Boston by water. And it was Dr. Warren who gave Paul Revere the word that it was time to make the attempt to reach Lexington with the warning for Sam Adams and John Hancock that the redcoats were coming.

Under cover of darkness, Revere crossed the Charles River in a rowboat, and in Charlestown he learned that Colonel Conant had seen "a glimmer and then a gleam of light" from the two lanterns hanging in the tall steeple of the Old North (Christ) Church in Boston, the signal that the British were leaving by water.

By eleven o'clock that night, Paul Revere was booted and spurred, and off in the moonlight on his immortal ride. He "alarmed almost every house" until he came to Lexington, and there he found Sam Adams and John Hancock, and warned them that close to a thousand redcoats were coming.

The two patriot leaders had already fled when the scarlet-coated troops marched into Lexington early in the morning of April 19. Waiting for them on the village green near Buckman's Tavern was a ragged line of about seventy minutemen. No order to fire was given, but suddenly a shot rang out, and then a volley from the redcoats. In the brief encounter, eight minutemen were killed and ten wounded.

By midmorning the British were in Concord, and there, in a skirmish at Concord Bridge, the embattled farmers "fired the shot heard round the world." The redcoats ran, and soon they were in full retreat, back through Lexington, and on toward Boston. Hundreds of infuriated patriots, alarmed and aroused, lay in wait along the way. Their deadly fire came from houses and barns, from behind trees and hedges and stone walls. The British lost 273 men in the bloody gauntlet they ran that day, the Americans 95.

On April 24, 1775, a weary, travel-stained rider swung off his horse in front of the City Tavern in Philadelphia and stunned the people with news of Lexington and Concord. The first blood of the Revolution had been shed. Muffled, the Bell tolled, and with each stroke of the great clapper, it was as if it mournfully intoned: Lexington . . . Concord . . . Lexington . . . Concord.

When the delegates returned to Philadelphia for the opening of the Second Continental Congress on May 10, they found the city astir with preparations for war. Companies in colorful uniforms drilled morning and evening. There were battalions that made a "most elegant appearance" in brown-and-white uniforms with white leather belts crossed over the breast. There were even companies of young Quakers who responded to the order, "Shoulder thy firelock."

The quarrel with the mother country that now threatened armed conflict had split the Society of Friends. They had approved the measures adopted for securing redress of grievances, but most of the Quakers refused to take up arms, and remained steadfastly loyal to King George. Those who seceded from the Society and gave their allegiance to the patriot cause were given the name of Free Quakers. They were generally called Fighting Quakers by the people.

The setting for the Second Continental Congress was the beautiful white-paneled Assembly Room in the State House on Chestnut Street. The provincial legislators held their meetings elsewhere in the building while the Congress was in session. The most distinguished of the few new delegates was Benjamin Franklin, who had been joyously welcomed upon his return home on May 5. He was now sixty-nine years old, and his body had been weakened by long years of service, but he took his seat in the Congress as a representative of Pennsylvania. Plainly dressed in a brown suit, he sat relaxed and composed with knees crossed and eyes often atwinkle behind little round spectacles. He wore no wig, and his thinning gray hair fell back from a high forehead onto his shoulders.

John Hancock had come for the first time with the delegation from Massachusetts. He was thirty-eight years old, quite tall and slender, and beginning to stoop a little. Handsome and always elegantly attired from his curled and powdered wig to the shining buckles on his shoes, he was vain, exceedingly ambitious, and eager for applause. But he had served the patriots well, and had done much good with his fortune. He succeeded Peyton Randolph as President of the Congress, and was an able and conscientious presiding officer.

Colonel Washington, calm and reserved in manner as always, was there again in uniform, a black cockade in his hat and a sword at his side. The Adamses were back, too, hopeful that the Congress would take decisive action—particularly, that it would accept responsibility for the army spread out in makeshift camps in a great crescent facing Boston.

After Lexington and Concord, this motley volunteer army had gathered in Cambridge across the Charles River from Boston. It was ill-fed, poorly clothed, and flimsily sheltered, but the minutemen—farmers, tradesmen, and mechanics—had laid siege to Boston, and now had General Gage and his redcoats penned up there. The Whigs had streamed out, the Tories had streamed in, and the rebel army across the river had virtually blockaded the town.

But the Congress was slow to take action, and John Adams fumed. The conservative majority, led by John Dickinson, was determined to make yet another effort to settle differences with the mother country amicably. Toward the end of May, Dickinson moved that "An Humble and Dutiful Petition" be sent to His Majesty. For the sake of unity, all the delegates voted for it, and some weeks later the "Olive Branch Petition," as John Adams called it, was sent to King George.

The critical situation of the army in Cambridge finally became evident to the most conservative of the delegates, and in the middle of June, George Washington was unanimously chosen "Supreme Commander of the forces raised and to be raised in defense of American liberty." He accepted the appointment with admirable modesty and sincerity. "I do not think myself equal to the command I am honored with," he said. "However, as the Congress desire, I will enter upon the momentous duty and exert every power I possess in their service."

A few days before Washington's departure, another prominent Virginian came from the House of Burgesses to take his place as a delegate to the Congress. Thomas Jefferson had made the trip from Williamsburg in a phaeton, accompanied by two servants. At thirty-two, he was tall, lean, and square-shouldered—"a straight-up man," as one of his servants described him. His fair skin was freckled, his gray-blue eyes wide-spaced, and his sandy reddish hair was brushed back and tied low on the neck with a ribbon.

On Friday, the twenty-third of June, General Washington and his military entourage left Philadelphia on the journey northward to Cambridge. It was a fine day with a brisk, cooling breeze, and with the band playing martial music and crowds cheering, the cavalcade was escorted a short distance by a troop of light horse in uniform and officers of the militia. Jefferson was probably one of the many delegates, along with those from Massachusetts, who rode out to see the General off.

Within hours after Washington had left the city, a dusty messenger galloped in with news of Bunker Hill. Again General Gage had finally been forced to take action. And again the patriots had learned about his plans before they were put into operation. The Massachusetts troops in Cambridge moved swiftly to Charlestown Peninsula and erected a forty-foot-square redoubt on Breed's Hill, to the southeast of Bunker Hill. Farther down the hill, a little fort of fence rails filled in with hay and grass was also thrown up.

It was from behind the redoubt and the rail fence that brave defenders repulsed wave after wave of redcoats with punishing fire on the hot, sunny afternoon of June 17. Finally, with their ammunition spent, they were forced to retreat. With rocks, broken muskets, and their bare fists, they fought "from one fence or wall to another" until they were driven off the peninsula. For the British, it was the kind of victory they did not want again. One thousand of their men were killed or wounded as against four hundred Americans, and they had seen that the stouthearted rebels could fight—not only Indian fashion behind trees and stone walls, but in the open and under continuous attack by disciplined troops.

In Philadelphia, Thomas Jefferson had settled down for the summer sessions of the Congress. He had found lodgings with a cabinetmaker named Benjamin Randolph, and in the company of other delegates Jefferson took dinner and supper at the City Tavern. In the little free time he had from congressional duties, he explored the shops and bought a variety of things, including books and music. And he drew the ingenious design from which his landlord made a small, slant-top writing box for him—plain, neat, convenient, and taking little room on a table, Jefferson said of it.

Unlike his fellow Virginians, Patrick Henry and Richard Henry Lee, Thomas Jefferson was not an eloquent speaker, and was usually silent in debate. He was a learned man, a scholar who could express himself best on paper. On committees and in conversation, he was "prompt, frank, and decisive," John Adams wrote, and said that he "soon seized upon my heart." It became a friendship that lasted throughout their lives. The young Virginian was also early drawn to the learned and modest Dr. Franklin.

Having come to the Congress with "a reputation for literature and science, and a happy talent for composition," Jefferson was soon serving on committees entrusted with the drafting of important papers. Only a few days after he had taken his seat, he had a hand in writing the spirited "Declaration on the Necessity of Taking Up Arms."

Benjamin Franklin was another member who rarely spoke in the Congress. Through Poor Richard he had said, "Here comes the orator with his flood of words and his drop of wisdom." Franklin found some relief from the oppressive July heat by composing a letter to William Strahan of London, an old friend whom he had formerly addressed as Straney. He wrote:

MR. STRAHAN:

You are a member of Parliament, and one of that majority which has doomed my country to destruction. You have begun to burn our towns and murder our people. Look upon your hands! They are stained with the blood of your relations. You and I were long friends. You are now my enemy, and

I am yours,
B. FRANKLIN

Little was accomplished by the sixty-odd delegates as the hot summer wore on and nerves became frayed. No one was as impatient with the endless petitions and addresses as John Adams. But he admitted that "like a coach and six, the swiftest horses must be slackened, and the slowest quickened, that all may keep an even pace." Sam Adams, blessed with great reserves of patience, counseled that it was better to wait "till the fruit is ripe before we gather it," and worked "to remove old prejudices, to instruct the unenlightened, convince the doubting, and fortify the timid."

Probably none of the weary delegates, passing through the center hall of the State House or walking in the Yard, looked up to where the Bell hung in the high, precarious steeple. Possibly not one of them even knew of the inscription around its crown that Isaac Norris had ordered for it back in 1751. And

Isaac Norris was not there to tell them about it, for he had died in July 1766. But the Bell was there, and it would ring out—it would ring out to proclaim liberty though the steeple might fall!

V

The Bell's Great Moment

FOR AMERICANS in the thirteen British colonies, 1776 was the year of decision. Relations with England had steadily deteriorated since the bitter quarrels with the mother country began with passage of the Stamp Act in 1765. The colonists had protested vigorously, had fearlessly asserted their rights, and had refused to be coerced by unjust measures.

They had no quarrel with the British people, and they were staunchly loyal to King George. They blamed Parliament and the King's ministers for their troubles, and they were confident that somehow the differences would be resolved—that King George would not fail them. The sentimental attachment of most Americans to the mother country was such that they had no thought of separation as a way out of an increasingly difficult situation. In March 1775, Benjamin Franklin declared he had never heard an American "drunk or sober" express a desire for permanent separation from England.

Even after Lexington and Concord, the majority still clung to hope of reconciliation. In May, Thomas Jefferson wrote that he would rather "be in dependence on Great Britain, properly limited, than on any other nation." But he added that rather than submit to the rights of the British Parliament to make laws for the colonies, he would lend his hand "to sink the whole island in the ocean." George Washington was a moderate when he took command of the army at Cambridge, and still hoped a break with England could be avoided. Among the patriot leaders, only Sam and John Adams were ready to take a stand for independence in the spring and summer of 1775.

It was not long before Americans learned how little good King George cared for them—how angrily determined he was to crush them. The Olive Branch Petition had been almost their last hope, and the King treated it with utter contempt, refusing to negotiate with the "illegal" Continental Congress. Then, early in January 1776, word came of the

King's speech to Parliament in which he had spoken angrily of the disturbance in the colonies as a "desperate conspiracy" on the part of insolent subjects, whose intention was to establish an independent empire.

Dire news of the passage of the Prohibitory Act quickly followed. It was in effect a declaration of war, for it proclaimed that the colonies were no longer under British protection. There would be a blockade of American ports from Maine to Georgia, and American ships would be seized. Even more shocking was the report that foreign soldiers would be sent over to reinforce the British army.

Independence had heretofore been a fearful word, a word so fraught with dreadful uncertainties that the people did not have the courage to utter it. Even now, with the colonies cut off from the mother country by an act of Parliament, there were many waverers who hung back, afraid to speak out boldly for separation.

It was not an American but a stranger from England who worked a "powerful change on the minds of people." Thomas Paine had come to Philadelphia late in the year of 1774, bearing a letter of introduction from Benjamin Franklin, who was then serving as colonial agent in London. Of humble birth, Paine had been a failure in business and in his personal life, but he was a gifted writer and a lover of freedom.

In America he found the times ripe for the kind of propaganda he could write with inspired eloquence. The result was the publication in January 1776 of a pamphlet of forty-seven pages entitled *Common Sense*. It was an immediate sensation. Within three months, 120,000 copies had been sold at two shillings a copy, and the total sales were reported to have been half a million.

The pamphlet was simply written and charged with emotional fervor. George III, the "royal brute of Britain," was more to be blamed for America's troubles than his ministers and Parliament, Paine wrote. And he urged: "O ye that love mankind, stand forth! Ye that dare oppose not only tyranny but the tyrant, stand forth!" He called for immediate independence, and declared that the cause of America was that of all mankind. It was absurd, he said, that an island should rule a continent, and on the last page of *Common Sense* there appeared in print for the first time the daring words: "The Free and Independent States of America."

Paine's stirring pamphlet released people from their fear of discussing independence openly and publicly. They were no longer afraid to speak out on the burning question of separation from Great Britain. It was bitterly debated in taverns and clubs, on the streets and on public platforms, and in the newspapers. There were still the timid who argued that independence would surely bring disaster. But many others were coming to believe it was worth the risks—that the only choice left was that of subjection to a tyrannical monarch or the fight for freedom.

The Continental Congress was no longer a temporary convention, meeting for a few months and then adjourning until called again, but a permanent body of representatives who were trying to run a war and govern a country.

Late in March there was a pause in the fierce debating over the issue of independence when the heartening news of the evacuation of Boston by the British troops reached Philadelphia. In a surprise move, Washington had fortified the two hills that overlooked the harbor to the southwest with cannon that had been sledded from Fort Ticonderoga to Cambridge. Threatened with bombardment, General William Howe, who had succeeded Gage, evacuated his troops and a thousand Tories, and on March 17 the British fleet sailed out of the harbor. No one rejoiced more than Sam Adams. The hated redcoats had at last been driven from his beloved town.

In the Congress, John Adams, the "main pillar in debate," led the fight against the moderates who refused to give up hope of reconciliation—against John Dickinson, Robert Morris, and James Wilson of Philadelphia; James Duane and John Jay of New York; and the Rutledge brothers, Edward and John, of South Carolina.

No argument could persuade these men that there

was nothing to be gained by further appeals to King George. But they were losing ground against the rising tide for independence. In May, John Adams scored a triumph when the Congress adopted his Preamble and Resolve urging the colonies to suppress all royal authority and to form governments of their own. Jubilant, he could report that every day by every post, "Independence rolls in upon us like a torrent."

About the middle of May, Thomas Jefferson returned to Philadelphia to take his seat again in the Congress. He went back to his old lodgings, but a week later moved to the new house of a bricklayer, a young married man named Jacob Graff. The three-story brick house was at the southwest corner of High and Seventh streets in an area where there were few other houses. Jefferson had the entire second floor, which consisted of a bedroom and a parlor with a passageway and the stairs between.

The colonies were setting up their own governments now, and one by one they began to authorize their representatives to vote for a declaration of independence. The Virginians matched the leadership of the Massachusetts men by taking a bolder step. On May 15, at a convention in Williamsburg, they had adopted a resolution that not only authorized their delegates in Philadelphia to vote for independence but also instructed them to *declare* for independence.

On Friday, the seventh of June, Richard Henry Lee—slim, aristocratic, and eloquent—rose before the Congress and asked leave to propose a resolution "according to the instructions of my constituents." With the eyes of every delegate riveted upon him, he slowly read from the paper in his hand:

> Resolved, That these United Colonies are, and of right ought to be, free and independent States; that they are absolved from all allegiance to the British Crown; and that all political connection between them and the State of Great Britain is, and ought to be, totally dissolved.

Before Lee sat down, plump little John Adams bounced to his feet and seconded the motion. But there was an anguished cry from the conciliation men—from those who represented the middle colonies and South Carolina. Thomas Jefferson, tolerant and patient, observed that they "were not matured enough for falling from the parent stem." It would be prudent, he suggested, to postpone the final decision until the first of July. And on Monday morning, June 10, all agreed that this should be done.

All the delegates agreed, too, that a declaration of independence should be prepared in the meantime. Not even the conciliators wanted to see such an important document "huddled up in a hurry." The next day, on June 11, a committee of five men was appointed to prepare a draft of a formal declaration—Jefferson, John Adams, Franklin, Robert Livingston of New York, and Roger Sherman of Connecticut.

Benjamin Franklin was the obvious choice of the one who should write it, since he was best known as a writer both in America and in Europe. But, reportedly, he was passed over by the committee because they feared he would put a joke in the document. And no one would have appreciated that more than Franklin himself. John Adams said bluntly he should have a minor part because he was feared and hated in the Congress. In the end, it was young Thomas Jefferson who was entrusted with the writing of the Declaration of Independence.

He wrote it in the little parlor of his second-floor lodgings on High Street, undisturbed by the noise of traffic—of drays and wagons rattling over the cobbles in the busy part of town near the wharves. Seated before a plain table on which he had placed his writing box, Jefferson worked with meticulous care, filling the pages with his small, neat script.

Later, he said that he consulted no book or pamphlet. But he had no need of reference materials, for this scholarly man who cherished liberty above all else had long reflected upon the rights and grievances of the colonies, and upon the "detestable and insupportable tyranny" of George III. Jefferson's purpose was clear. The American patriots should be justified in the stand for independence that they were compelled to take, and the Declaration should express their thoughts. He did not look for new principles or new arguments. His intention was "to place before mankind the common sense of the subject."

The Declaration was finished a few days before a decision on the question of independence itself had been reached. Having approved Jefferson's document, the committee submitted it to the Congress on June 28. There, in the State House, the great debate was approaching the climax. The advocates of independence had made a supreme effort to win the support of all the delegates. It was of vital importance that the Congress should act for all the colonies—that there should be a united independent America.

The final exchange of bitter words came from John Dickinson and John Adams on the afternoon of July 1. The sky had darkened and candles had been lighted when Dickinson made his last plea. In a voice choked with emotion, he warned that separation from Great Britain would be like "destroying our house in winter before we have got another shelter."

While John Adams spoke in rebuttal, the storm broke, and he had to raise his voice to make himself heard above the roll of thunder and rain beating against the windowpanes. No record of his speech was kept, but Jefferson said afterward that he came out "with a power of thought and expression that moved us from our seats."

The next morning the delegates met to take the final vote. It was Tuesday, July 2, a gray day with overcast skies. Dickinson and Robert Morris stayed away, and at last Pennsylvania came out for independence. South Carolina capitulated, and Caesar Rodney, after an eighty-mile ride in darkness and rain, arrived just in time to swing Delaware over to the affirmative side. Twelve colonies voted to adopt the resolution of independence that had been presented by Richard Henry Lee, and New York's vote was promised at a later date.

In the late afternoon of that same day, July 2, the delegates began their critical reading of the Declaration. The room was hot, and from a livery stable across the street horseflies flew in and stung the distinguished gentlemen through their white silk stockings. But it was the criticism of his work that made Jefferson writhe with discomfort.

Dr. Franklin, sitting close by, tried to comfort him by relating the story of a hatter who asked several friends for their opinions of a sign he had designed for his shop. Each suggested dropping a different word, and finally there was nothing left except the hatter's name and the picture of a hat. Years later, Jefferson himself could joke about his ordeal. His Declaration went through the Congress much faster, he said, because of the horseflies.

On July 4, the delegates completed the editing of the great document, and on that day it was adopted by twelve colonies, while the New York representatives refrained from voting. Jefferson had suffered needlessly from the critical examination of his composition. Actually, it was strengthened rather than weakened by the revisions, mainly deletions, that the Congress made.

The Declaration of Independence is roughly divided into four parts. In the preamble, or introduction, the purpose of the document is stated. Then comes the paragraph in which the author speaks not for Americans alone, but for all mankind in his lofty statement of the rights of every human being. It begins with the well-known words that have never lost, by repetition and familiarity, their freshness and uplifting appeal:

> We hold these truths to be self-evident, that all men are created equal, that they are endowed by their Creator with certain unalienable Rights, that among these are Life, Liberty and the pursuit of Happiness.

Moreover, the purpose of governments is to secure these rights for the governed. They exist not to use men—not to tyrannize over them—but to serve them. That is the function of governments, and they should "derive their just powers from the consent of the governed."

The Americans had enjoyed no such rights under King George. Instead, his rule "has been a history of repeated injuries," and for the purpose of establishing "an absolute tyranny over these states." In proof of this, twenty specific charges are listed in the third part of the Declaration. And they are directed not against the British people or Parliament, but against the King.

The Declaration closes, in its fourth part, with the actual declaration of independence, including Richard Henry Lee's resolution that was adopted on July 2. Clearly and simply written, it is a moving and exalted expression of Jefferson's profound concern for the rights of all mankind—"a stately and passionate chant of human freedom."

When the Declaration of Independence was adopted, Sam Adams was fifty-four years old, and he had lived to see his lifelong dream of an independent America realized. He had neglected his own affairs to dedicate his life to the cause of freedom. The earliest and most active of the pre-Revolutionary agitators, he never sought the limelight, preferring to work behind the scenes and let others have the glory and the applause. He left no record as an eloquent public speaker, and no paper that he ever wrote has been preserved as an important document. But with "cheerful spirit and inflexible will," Sam Adams did more than anyone else for American rights and liberties, and in the years, too, when the flame of opposition to the King and royal governors burned low. Perhaps the finest tribute to this great patriot came from Jefferson, who said that he was "truly the Man of the Revolution."

With the drafting of the final form of the Declaration completed, the Congress immediately ordered it authenticated and printed. President John Hancock affixed his bold signature, and it was also signed by the Secretary, Charles Thomson. Then it was rushed to John Dunlap, who printed it that night of July 4 on a broadside.

Since the New York delegation had refrained from the final vote, it was entitled "A Declaration by the Representatives of the United States in General Congress Assembled." It was not until July 15, when the Congress received the resolution of the New York convention, that it became the "Unanimous Declaration." On August 2, the copy that Timothy Matlack had engrossed on parchment was signed by most of the fifty-six men who were at that time members of the Congress. Those who were absent on this historic occasion signed later.

The momentous decision to adopt the resolution of independence was made on July 2. This was the day that John Adams believed would be "the most memorable in the history of America." But from the beginning, Americans chose to celebrate July 4 as the birthday of the nation—the day on which twelve states agreed to the written Declaration that embodied the resolution.

Not all the people in the newly created nation rejoiced with the patriots (Whigs) over independence. There were many loyalists (Tories), particularly among the more prosperous people in the North, who bitterly opposed separation from the mother country. The patriots took an oath of loyalty to their country, and the loyalists, who refused to do so, were treated as traitors. Large numbers of them joined forces with the British and at one time or another fought against their own countrymen in the Revolution.

But news of the adoption of the Declaration of Independence was wildly and joyously celebrated in each of the thirteen states. The Congress had ordered that copies of the document be sent with all haste to the various assemblies and conventions, to the committees of safety, and to the commanding officers of the Continental troops. Swift post riders set off on July 5 from the City Tavern in Philadelphia with broadsides for distribution, but it took many days to reach distant points of the country.

Appropriately, the first broadside was received by the Committee of Safety in the city that was the birthplace of the nation. Because there had to be time for planning the celebration of so momentous an event, the Declaration was not proclaimed in Philadelphia until three days later. The full text of the document was printed on the first page of all the city's newspapers—in the *Evening Post,* the *Packet,* the *Gazette,* the *Journal,* and the *Ledger.*

The Bell's great moment came at noon on Monday, the eighth of July 1776. Slowly, and with deep-throated chant, it fulfilled its destiny by proclaiming liberty "throughout all the land unto all the inhabitants thereof." And from Christ Church belfry, from St. Peter's and St. Joseph's, and from Lutheran and Presbyterian steeples, the church bells chimed in with peals of rejoicing.

In the warm sunshine of that memorable day, processions formed and the streets filled with people. The constables, the sheriff, the Mayor, members of the Assembly, and others prominent in civic affairs fell into line with the military. The Committee of Inspection met first at Philosophical Hall, then joined the Committee of Safety at the Lodge, and along with other groups marched to the State House Yard, where a great crowd of people had gathered.

The ceremony centered upon a circular railed platform that had been erected by the American Philosophical Society for astronomical observation. Here Colonel John Nixon, an ardent patriot and member of the Committee of Safety, stood with a copy of the Declaration in his hand. Standing just below the platform were members of the Congress and the Assembly, and stretching back to the farthest limits of the Yard were the people packed close together.

The last echoes of the Bell faded away, and Colonel Nixon, tall and robust, began to read the Declaration of Independence in a clear, strong voice. There were probably few in the crowd who appreciated the beauty of the language or the lofty sentiments that the words expressed. What the people were really celebrating that day was independence itself, not the document that was a declaration of it. But those fateful last words told them what lay ahead.

The farmers, mechanics, small shopkeepers, carpenters, painters, plasterers, sailors, ropewalkers, shipwrights—and yes, perhaps Pass and Stow whose names were on the Bell—knew what it meant "to pledge to each other our lives, our fortunes, and our sacred honor." To all the plain people assembled there it meant they were celebrating independence then, but they would have to fight for it. And three mighty cheers "rended the welkin."

The celebrations lasted the rest of the day and most of the night. To the ringing of bells and the firing of salutes, battalions paraded on the Common, and King George's arms, which had been ripped from the State House door, were brought there by a triumphant crowd. That night the British Lion and the Unicorn were consumed by the flames of a huge bonfire.

At the ceremony held in the State House Yard that day, Thomas Jefferson's name was not mentioned. It was his Declaration of Independence that was read, but he was not called to the platform to be honored as its author. No one pointed to the steeple, either, and said: "Up there hangs the great Bell. You have heard its voice, too, ring out for freedom."

Both Jefferson and the Bell had to wait for the honors that later would come to them for proclaiming liberty for all men.

VI

Washington's Victory at Trenton

GENERAL WASHINGTON did not tarry long in Boston after the departure of the British on March 17, 1776. Feeling certain that Howe would return soon to attempt the capture of New York City, he brought his Continental troops there in the middle of April. They found the soldiers already stationed in Manhattan hard at work digging trenches, chopping down trees, and erecting barricades and earthworks.

Recognizing that the city, surrounded by navigable water, was indefensible, Washington added fortifications on Long Island across the East River from New York, and strengthened the defenses at Fort Washington on the northern end of Manhattan Island, and at Fort Lee over on the Jersey shore. Strategic hills bristled with redoubts and batteries, and obstructions to the passage of ships were stretched across the Hudson River.

But Staten Island was left undefended. It lay to the southwest of Long Island, and was separated from it by the Narrows, a strait that connected the Lower with the Upper Bay. On July 2, the very day on which the Congress in Philadelphia voted for separation from Great Britain, General William Howe and thousands of British regulars from Halifax landed on Staten Island. Ten days later, the General's older brother, Admiral Lord Howe, came in with his battle fleet. For the rest of the summer, and into the fall, Lower New York Bay swarmed with transports bringing in redcoats and Hessians, the German soldiers Britain had hired. The number finally swelled to about 34,000 well-equipped troops.

Washington had appealed to both New York and New Jersey for more men, and by late August his forces had risen in numbers to 20,000, but many of them were militia. The American armies had two kinds of troops. The Continentals, or regulars, signed up for a year, and these were the soldiers who became the backbone of the Revolution. The militia were state troops who came and went at will—the "rabble in arms," largely untrained and unreliable.

Bracing himself to ward off the British assault, Washington had sent 8,000 soldiers to Long Island. Some of them manned the fortified line on Brooklyn Heights, but most of the troops were stationed along a ridge to the southward to hold off the expected British advance against the fortifications.

Although the position of the Americans was precarious, Howe hesitated to move quickly and boldly against New York. Since the British attack upon the southern colonies had already failed, he had lost his earlier confidence in an easy victory over Washington. Now he let the weeks of good summer weather slip by while he thought of all the difficulties that might lie ahead. At last he reached the decision to send his British and German regulars into action on Long Island.

Before the sun rose on the morning of August 22, they were being ferried by the thousands across the Narrows and landed near Gravesend. The attack on the American force along the ridge came on the morning of the twenty-seventh, in front and on their unprotected left flank. The patriot soldiers fought gallantly and desperately; but, outnumbered and outflanked, they suffered crushing defeat, with casualties of 2,000, and half that number captured along with two major generals.

Those who escaped retreated to the entrenchments on Brooklyn Heights. When Washington heard of the defeat of his troops, he promptly, and unaccountably, crossed the East River with six regiments of reinforcements and took command of the forces on Long Island.

Fortunately, Howe was, as usual, slow to press his advantage. He did not storm the patriot fortifications at once, as his officers urged him to do, and this gave Washington time to realize the grave peril of his position. A regiment composed of fishermen from Marblehead, Massachusetts, crossed the East River, and, on a night of rain and wind, assisted in evacuating all the Long Island troops in small boats to Manhattan. The British knew nothing about the daring operation until the fog lifted the following morning.

Safe for the moment with his army gathered on Manhattan, Washington debated what to do next. The morale of his men was so low that there was a contagion of "cannon fever" among the militia, and many of them "very prudently skulked home." Howe had no such difficulty with his well-disciplined troops, and Washington's little "fleet" of schooners, sloops, and whaleboats posed no threat to the Admiral's warships.

But even with all the advantage on his side, the younger Howe took no action after his victory on Long Island until finally, on September 12, Washington began the withdrawal of his army from New York City to Harlem Heights in the northern part of Manhattan Island. Then the dilatory British General sent detachments of his regulars in pursuit. The patriot army escaped, and Washington bitterly described his retreat as "disgraceful and dastardly." Howe took possession of New York City, and having decided the war could not be won in 1776, spent a month making the city secure against the retreating patriots.

For the dispirited Americans, retreating had only begun. On October 12, the cautious Howe resumed the offensive. He sailed with a large force up the East River, then farther up Long Island Sound, and landed near New Rochelle in Westchester. Having decided that Manhattan Island could not be held, and believing it was Howe's intention to encircle his forces, Washington withdrew from Harlem Heights. With 14,000 men he retreated northward to White Plains. The British caught up with the American commander there, and on October 28 won a minor victory. Washington then moved to a more defensible position at North Castle, and Howe dug in on the hill he had taken.

No great losses had been suffered by the patriots in these moves, and with the approach of winter it seemed likely there would be a lull in the fighting until spring. It soon became evident, however, that Howe would not spend the winter on the hill he had captured near White Plains, nor would he return at once to his base in New York City. Alarmed by the march westward of the British troops, Washington made the desperate decision to leave part of his army at North Castle, and a small force at Peekskill to guard the Hudson, while he hurried with the remainder to Fort Lee.

The patriot garrison of 3,000 men at Fort Washington had not been withdrawn when he evacuated Manhattan, and a force of 4,500 still held Fort Lee across the Hudson in New Jersey. Unknown to the American commander, the plan of Fort Washington and the weakness of its defenses had been revealed to Howe by a deserter. And on November 16, Washington and the commandant at Fort Lee had to look on helplessly while the fort across the river fell before an overwhelming assault by British and Hessian troops. Four days later, Fort Lee was left to the advancing regiments of Lord Cornwallis, and its garrison joined Washington in his retreat into New Jersey.

Instead of following up his victories by driving hard upon the heels of Washington and his broken and dwindling army, Howe decided to get ready to go into winter quarters. He ordered Lord Cornwallis to pursue Washington and drive him only beyond New Brunswick. Thus some of the British troops could be quartered for the winter in eastern New Jersey and would be in a good position to start the next campaign the following spring.

Meanwhile, Washington had pushed on to Newark, and was making frantic appeals to New Jersey for militia, and to the Congress in Philadelphia for troops and supplies of all kinds. On November 29, the British vanguard under Cornwallis marched into Newark just as Washington's rear guard was leaving on the opposite side of the town in a forced retreat to New Brunswick. Fortunately, as the ragged patriot troops slogged on in imminent danger of being overtaken, Cornwallis slowed down, giving the American commander time to cross the Delaware River and reach the west bank. Then Washington hurriedly collected all the boats for many miles on both sides of Trenton, so that he controlled passage to the Pennsylvania side.

Faced with this difficulty when he reached the river on the cold Sunday afternoon of December 8, Cornwallis decided it was time to go into winter quarters. His troops were billeted at posts, mainly at Bordentown and Trenton, on the Delaware's east bank, and at the advance base in New Brunswick.

But in this bleak month of December 1776, Washington was not thinking of retiring to winter quarters. He was thinking of taking the offensive—of making a supreme effort to regain control of western New Jersey. His spirits had sunk low, but neither the disasters of the preceding months nor the shameful retreat had caused him to despair. He had made mistakes, and he had suffered humiliating defeats, but his courage and determination had not been shaken. Washington was never stronger, or more admirable, than in adversity, and it was this and his rigid self-discipline that set him apart from ordinary men.

The British drive toward Philadelphia had alarmed the people. They were jittery—almost in a panic. The Continental Congress had wisely departed and taken refuge in Baltimore. The Bell was silent. But Tom Paine was as busy in defense of the patriot cause with his quill pen as he had been when he wrote *Common Sense*.

Now the first of his series of pamphlets called *The Crisis* was ready for distribution. It began with the memorable lines:

> These are the times that try men's souls: The summer soldier and the sunshine patriot will, in this crisis, shrink from the service of his country; but he that stands it NOW deserves the love and thanks of man and woman.

This and successive issues of *The Crisis* lifted the morale of both the people and the patriot soldiers. American officers read each number to their men as it appeared.

Washington had decided upon the daring plan of recrossing the Delaware on Christmas night and attacking Trenton before daylight. He had the boats, but he knew he must get across the river before it froze. His army had been strengthened by the arrival of the troops from Peekskill, and Thomas Mifflin, a patriotic Fighting Quaker, had raised 2,000 militiamen in Philadelphia.

At six o'clock on Christmas evening, the patriot regiments marched down to a ferry above Trenton. One of Washington's aides recorded in his diary: "It is fearfully cold and raw, and a snowstorm is setting in. It will be a terrible night for the soldiers who have no shoes. Some of them have tied old rags around their feet; others are barefoot, but I have not heard a man complain."

Nine hours later, at 3:00 A.M. on December 26, the diarist wrote:

> I am writing in the ferry house. The troops are all over, and the boats have gone back for the artillery. We are three hours behind the set time. The men have had a hard time forcing the boats through the floating ice with the snow drifting in their faces. I have never seen Washington so determined as he is now. He stands on the bank of the river, wrapped in his cloak, superintending the landing of his troops. He is calm and collected, but very determined. The storm is changing to sleet and cuts like a knife. The last cannon is being landed, and we are ready to mount our horses.

At bitter dawn, Washington's troops struck suddenly and unexpectedly. Colonel Johann Rall had not carried out an order to build fortifications, and he and his Hessian soldiers were asleep after having celebrated a German Christmas. Rall made a brave but futile attempt to organize resistance. In the brief fight he was mortally wounded, and most of his men were taken prisoners. The patriot troops also took more than a thousand muskets, six cannon, and other military stores. Their own losses were slight.

When Cornwallis heard of Rall's defeat and death, he rushed over from New York with 6,000 British regulars. Washington narrowly escaped being trapped in Trenton, but he eluded Cornwallis, succeeded in reaching Princeton, where he engaged in a skirmish with the redcoats, and then marched to the hills of Morristown and at last settled down in winter quarters. Howe withdrew his forces to New Brunswick and other posts to the east.

After heartbreaking defeats, the American commander had realized his objective of retaking western New Jersey, and he had done it in a brilliant maneuver and with spectacular courage. From Philadelphia, a patriot wrote to the Congress in Baltimore: "The victory at Trenton has given such amazing spirit to our people. We have vast numbers of fine militia coming in momently."

VII

The Bell in Hiding

IN RECOGNITION OF his triumph on Long Island, Howe was knighted. And soon after the fall of Fort Washington, Sir William began correspondence with the War Office in London about plans for 1777. The breadth of the Atlantic made communication slow, and as the letters shuttled back and forth, and Howe changed his plans several times, months passed before a decision was finally reached.

The General was committed to the plan of invading Pennsylvania with himself in command of a large force. He had great hopes for the outcome of this invasion, for he believed the Tories would join the royal ranks in large numbers, making the conquest of the patriots and their army an easy one.

But the disposition of British regulars elsewhere, to fight if necessary while Sir William campaigned in Pennsylvania, created problems difficult to settle. The most difficult concerned the plan for another invading army. General John Burgoyne had gained approval of *his* plan to drive southward from Canada by way of Lake Champlain and the Hudson River to Albany, and thus to sever New England from the rest of the colonies.

There was prolonged discussion of how much support Burgoyne would need, but Sir William took no steps to cooperate with him. And the letter from London urging Howe to finish the Pennsylvania campaign in time to give the Canadian army whatever assistance it needed came too late.

Having at last decided to transport 11,000 redcoats by sea to the head of Chesapeake Bay and from there to lead them northward by land to Philadelphia, Howe dawdled for some weeks longer, and did not begin his preparations until June.

Meanwhile spring had come to New Jersey and Pennsylvania, and with it stirrings of hope and an infusion of vigor into Washington's army at Morristown. Continental recruits began to arrive, and by the end of May, 9,000 had joined the General's veterans. The Continental navy and the privateers were bringing in military stores from captured British vessels, and secret aid from France and Spain had begun to arrive—thousands of muskets, tons of powder, and large quantities of clothing and blankets. But Washington could not guess where Howe would move next. The American commander looked warily to the east and studied the intelligence reports that came in.

The Congress had returned to Philadelphia and to its sessions in the State House. June passed and July came, and still there was no cause for alarm. And on Friday, the Fourth of July, the city forgot the perils and terrors of war to celebrate "with demonstrations of joy and festivity" the first anniversary of the Declaration of Independence.

Bells answered bells—the bells of the Old Swedes' Church down by the Delaware, of St. Peter's, of Christ Church—until the chimes mingled and pealed together from all the steeples in the city. And deeper-sounding than all the rest, the Bell in the State House steeple rang out once more in celebration of the young country's first year of liberty—the Bell that was now just one year short of being a quarter-century old.

In the harbor, and along the river, armed ships and large galleys were drawn up before the city. Colored streamers rippled from yards and masts and rigging, and at one o'clock the seamen were ordered aloft to man the ships. Companies of men "drawn up in order in the air" made a striking spectacle. With every man in his place on yards and shrouds, and with the wharves and shore crowded with spectators, thirteen cannon shots boomed from each of the ships, and one from each of the thirteen galleys, in honor of the thirteen states of America.

At three o'clock in the afternoon, an elegant dinner was served at the City Tavern in honor of the members of the Congress. Among the other guests were army officers, public officials, civic leaders, and "strangers of eminence." The Hessian band that Washington had captured, along with other prisoners, at Trenton on December 26 was brought in and "heightened the festivities with some fine performances, suited to the joyous occasion." Following dinner, toasts were drunk, punctuated by volleys fired by a company of soldiers drawn up in front of the tavern.

In the evening, with the city "splendidly illuminated," there was an exhibition of fireworks on the Common, which began and ended with the firing of thirteen rockets. And with a last pealing of church bells, and a last reverberating clang from the Bell at the State House, Philadelphia's celebration of the first anniversary of independence was over.

A time that would, indeed, try men's souls lay just ahead. On the last day of July, Washington learned that the British fleet was off the capes of Delaware

Bay and apparently moving toward the Delaware River. But after he had moved his troops to a camp about twenty miles north of Philadelphia, dispatch riders came with the news that Howe's fleet had entered Chesapeake Bay. There was no longer any uncertainty about Sir William's plans. It was clear now that instead of marching overland to attack the city, he intended to land his forces at the head of Chesapeake Bay and march the fifty-five miles to Philadelphia.

During the months of inactivity, Washington's army had been further strengthened by Continentals and militia until it numbered close to 16,000 men. And a young major general who was destined for fame had joined the Commander's staff. The Marquis de Lafayette, fired with enthusiasm for the patriot cause, had come from France to offer his services, and the Congress had promptly commissioned him a major general. The gangling youth—tall, thin, big-shouldered, and just nineteen years old—was not physically attractive. His nose was sharp and prominent, and his scant reddish-brown hair could not conceal a receding forehead. But Lafayette's eagerness and charm made up for his homely appearance, and Washington was quickly drawn to him.

The Commander had no intention of leaving Philadelphia to its fate, and he now moved to place his army between the city and Howe's advancing redcoats. On the Sunday morning of August 24, between seven and ten o'clock, his confident troops marched through the city on their way to meet the enemy. Shabby uniforms had been freshened; each man wore a "green sprig, emblem of hope" in his hat; and drums and fifes played a "quick step." John Adams noted that "our soldiers don't step exactly in time, nor turn out their toes as they ought," but they marched bravely on to the Brandywine, and many of them never came back.

From Philadelphia, Washington led his troops south to Wilmington, Delaware. He lay encamped here until Howe began his march from the head of Chesapeake Bay on September 8, moving northwestward toward the Brandywine River. In a night march, Washington hurried over the hills to Chads Ford, where he crossed to the east side of the Brandywine. The most important road traversed the river here, and the American commander anticipated that the ensuing battle would be fought at and around this ford.

Hills rose along the eastern bank of the Brandywine, and there were three fords within a distance of five miles between Chads and the point at which the river forked into its east and west branches. On the east branch, just above the forks, was Buffington's Ford, and the last one that Washington tried to guard. Unfamiliar with the terrain, he had to depend on the information he could gather from others. And one of his generals assured him there were no other fords crossed by roads for twelve miles above Buffington's. As a matter of fact, there were two more over the east branch a few miles above Buffington's, with roads crossing them, one of which connected with a main road that crossed the west branch at still another ford.

Someone had accurately informed Sir William about these fords, and this proved to be vital to the outcome of the battle. He posted a detachment of Hessians on the hills along the west bank of the river facing the American concentration of forces at Chads Ford. Other patriot units were strung out for several miles above the ford, and the wooded heights below were held by the Pennsylvania militia. While the Hessian troops at Chads Ford engaged in desultory fighting to "amuse" the Americans, Howe went ahead with his strategy.

General Cornwallis, accompanied by Sir William, had marched off in a thick fog at dawn with 7,000 British regulars. Moving northward at first, about six miles from the nearest American troops along the Brandywine, he came to the fords above Buffington's, and in a perfectly executed flanking movement, crossed first the west fork and then the east fork of the river, and came down in the rear of the American forces.

In spite of the fog, Cornwallis's march was observed and reported. But the information Washington received was at first inconclusive and then contradictory. Just before two o'clock in the afternoon, after having given and reversed orders, he knew he had been trapped. An hour later, the Americans were fighting desperately to extricate themselves. What had come perilously close to catastrophic defeat for them became instead, by heroic resistance, a fairly orderly retreat.

At early dusk on that eleventh of September 1777, the Battle of Brandywine ended when Sir William ordered a halt to the fighting. Marching by night, Washington retreated to Chester and the river below Philadelphia. His casualties numbered upward of a thousand, those of the British about half that number. One of the American wounded was young Lafayette.

Howe did not pursue the retreating enemy. Satisfied, as he had been at other times, with the immediate victory, he decided to rest and take time to plan, slowly and methodically, the next move, rather than to drive ahead for more decisive results. So he stayed on for a while at Chads Ford, knowing that the road to Philadelphia had been opened and that he could proceed there at his usual leisurely pace.

Washington was not blamed for his defeat at Brandywine, and the Congress voted thirty hogsheads of rum to his army as a "compliment to their gallant behavior." The troops were now encamped at Germantown, five miles distant to the northwest, and in Philadelphia such measures as could be taken against the day of Howe's occupation of the city were pushed.

Hordes of citizens left to find refuge in other towns. A resident of Allentown noted in his diary: "Since the Battle of Brandywine many thousand wagons have passed my door, and are continually passing in great numbers. Every day some of the inhabitants of Philadelphia are coming up to settle here. The road from Easton and Reading by my house is now the most traveled street in America."

The Congress passed on an order to the Supreme Executive Council of the State of Pennsylvania "to appoint properly discreet persons to take into possession linens, blankets, other woolens, shoes, spirits, and other necessaries for the use of the army which they find in stores and warehouses in Philadelphia, and have the goods sent to some secure place to prevent their falling into the hands of the enemy."

And the bells—Philadelphia's bells must not fall into British hands to be converted into bullets that would take the lives of patriot soldiers! An order went out to the Commissary General of military stores to apply to the Council of Pennsylvania for permission to remove all public bells to a place of safety. And crews of strong workmen carefully lowered the bells of all the city's churches and placed them on waiting wagons.

The heaviest of all was the great Bell that hung

in the State House steeple. But it was brought down safely and roped securely on an open wagonbed. And now the Bell was ready for the first of the many journeys it would take.

Members of the Congress had already gone to Lancaster, Pennsylvania (later they would go to York), when the wagons carrying the bells joined Washington's long baggage train. There were 700 wagons, pulled by sturdy farm horses, in the train that snaked out from Philadelphia and rattled over the rough road northwestward to Reading. It was guarded by 200 soldiers under the command of Colonel William Polk of North Carolina.

At Reading the baggage train turned to the northeast and took the rugged, hilly road to Bethlehem, which lay in the beautiful Lehigh Valley. At a point near the descent to Luckenbach's mill, the wagon carrying the Bell broke down, and a transfer had to be made to another. Some of the wagons stopped at Bethlehem, and at a camp on the south side of the Lehigh River the army stores were unloaded and placed in safety in the town. The rest of the train went on to nearby Allentown for unloading and the storing of baggage here.

In Allentown, on September 24, 1777, the great Bell and the bells of Christ Church were lifted off the wagons and hidden under the floor of the Zion Reformed Church. Father Abraham Blumer, the minister, must have been there, fluttering anxiously about in his long black robes while husky men labored to get the heavy bells down into their hiding place without mishap. The church, replacing an earlier one, had been completed in 1776. It was a rectangular stone building, with double doors on each side of a projecting tower that rose just above a slanting roof.

On September 16, 1777, a Quaker lady of Philadelphia recorded in her journal: "Well! Here are the English in earnest. About 3,000 came in through Second Street without opposition or interruption."

The victorious, self-confident Sir William had at last realized his objective of taking the City of Brotherly Love, but when wise old Ben Franklin heard the news in Paris, he said, "No—Philadelphia has captured Howe."

It was not easy for an invading army of nearly 18,000 men to find shelter, but half the British troops were quartered in Germantown. In Philadelphia, the officers were billeted in wealthy homes, and the State House was filled with troops and the Yard with cannon.

At dusk on October 3, Washington made one more daring attempt to surprise the enemy and recoup his losses. He advanced under cover of darkness to Germantown from his camp at Skippack Creek, sixteen miles distant. The counterattack began at dawn, but the American commander was dogged by the same kind of ill-luck that had defeated him at Brandywine—by fog and such confusion that at a critical moment patriot soldiers in one column fired upon those in another.

Howe and his army could now settle down in the city, safe and comfortable for the winter. But the British conqueror had not received the joyous welcome he had expected, and a scant 300 Tories volunteered to join his army. In southeastern Pennsylvania loyalist sympathizers were fairly numerous, but most of them were Quakers whose only support was their willingness to sell foodstuffs to the British for hard cash. And in late October, Howe learned that the attempt of the Canadian army to isolate New England had failed. Finding himself surrounded and with his food supply running low, General John Burgoyne had surrendered his entire army at Saratoga, New York, on October 17, to General Horatio Gates.

In spite of the dismal news, Sir William spent a "rollicking winter" in Philadelphia. The prisoners he had taken at Brandywine and Germantown were herded into the old jail on Walnut Street, and many of them died and were buried in the potter's field. The long room on the second floor of the State House was used as a hospital for wounded American soldiers. Elsewhere there was nothing but gaiety. Howe and his officers were entertained by hospitable Tories; they attended weekly balls at the City Tavern; dined at the Indian Queen, enjoyed cockfights in Moore's Alley, and were diverted by plays at the theater.

It was a very different kind of winter for Washington at Valley Forge, twenty miles northwest of Philadelphia, where he brought his weary, hungry men to go into winter quarters. The campsite was a wooded slope about two miles long that took its name from the ruins of a forge the British troops had destroyed in September. They had also cleaned the area of food, but the hills and the curving sweep of the Schuylkill River in the rear of the camp provided natural protection.

There was plenty of wood, but it was green wood, and the fires burned fitfully. By Christmas most of the soldiers were still living miserably in tents and burrows, for in the bitter cold huts went up slowly, and there were not enough blankets to provide warmth against the icy winds that swept chillingly through the barren campsite. And while the British ate good beef, the Americans drank soup "full of burnt leaves and dirt." During that terrible winter, some 3,000 of the 11,000 men died of cold, privation, and disease.

But on a late February day, a foreigner came who must have seemed heaven-sent to Washington. Baron Friedrich von Steuben, stout and balding, was a Prussian officer who calmly took over the task of drilling and training the army of scarecrows. For the first time, American soldiers were put through the discipline of daily drills. Lacking a drill manual, Steuben wrote his own. And he not only drilled the soldiers himself in his guttural voice and with his limited command of English; he also successfully trained a company of drillmasters.

While the British in Philadelphia reveled in balls and ate the fat of the land, those who survived the sufferings of that winter on the bleak slopes along the Schuylkill grew tough. And Valley Forge became a symbol of the fortitude and endurance of the American soldier.

VIII

The Rising Nation

NEWS of General Burgoyne's surrender at Saratoga reached London on December 2, 1777. It was a staggering blow to British pride and British hopes of a quick victory over the Americans. Howe's success at Brandywine and his occupation of Philadelphia did little to dispel the gloom and the confusion, for Washington had escaped with most of his army intact. And the New Year would bring even more dispiriting news to the King and his ministers.

Benjamin Franklin had been in Paris since December 1776 trying to persuade the French and Louis XVI that it would be to their advantage to join the Americans as a military ally. He talked about how powerful France's old enemy, England, would be if she won the war against the patriots; about mutual trade benefits if America was victorious; and about liberty. It was easy enough for the sage of Philadelphia to charm the French. He became the idol of all classes, and at his house in the suburb of Passy entertained statesmen, scientists, and scholars. No other ambassador could have created so much good will for the United States.

But the French ministry and the King were hesitant. News of British advances and patriot retreats, and of Howe's capture of Philadelphia, made them cautious, fearful that the patriots were not strong enough to stand up to British might. And then on December 4 they heard about Saratoga. Two days after the English had been so dejected by news of the disaster to Burgoyne's army, the French heard it and were elated. They not only thought it worthwhile to give aid to the Americans, but were now convinced that there was not too much risk in helping them by taking up arms against Great Britain. On February 6, 1778, the treaty that brought France into the war as an ally of the patriots was signed.

This diplomatic victory for the Americans did not affect the plans of Sir William Howe in Philadelphia. He had been severely criticized in London, and knowing that he had failed to make the most of his opportunities, he had sent in his resignation to the War Office earlier in the year. It was accepted, and in May 1778 he was replaced by Sir Henry Clinton.

The new commander began preparations at once for the evacuation of the British troops in and around Philadelphia. The military stores were loaded on Admiral Howe's fleet of transports, and 3,000 Tories and most of the Hessians sailed away with the Admiral. After the departure of the fleet, Clinton withdrew his main forces swiftly and silently during the night of June 18.

Washington quickly left Valley Forge in pursuit, and the patriot army overtook the British at Monmouth Courthouse in New Jersey. An indecisive battle was fought here on June 28, and without heavy losses on either side. Clinton marched on to New York. Washington led his army to a temporary camp in New Brunswick, and on the sizzling Fourth of July they celebrated the second anniversary of the Declaration of Independence. The troops paraded, the artillery discharged thirteen cannon, and in the evening "His Excellency and the gentlemen and ladies had a ball at headquarters with great pomp."

In Philadelphia there was a brave display of fireworks but not much else. The bells had not been returned, and the citizens were trying to restore cleanliness and order to their city after nine months of occupation by the redcoats. There had been more destruction of property and cutting down of trees in the suburbs to the north. What the people in the city found most offensive was the "abominable odor."

The State House, particularly, was "in a most filthy condition and the inside much torn to pieces." And a large pit had been dug close by into which not only filth of all kinds had been thrown, but also dead horses. The Congress returned and took quarters elsewhere until the work of cleaning, painting, and restoration in the State House was completed. Sometime in that summer of 1778, the bells were brought back to the city from Allentown, but there is no record of the date on which the great Bell was hung again in the State House steeple.

Philadelphia had seen the last of the British troops and of the convivial Sir William Howe. And after the arrival of the French fleet in American waters in July 1778, there was no more large-scale fighting in the northern and middle states. Between that year and 1780, Washington kept his men spread out in camps from West Point on the Hudson to Morristown, New Jersey. Wherever the American commander was stationed, he had to cope daily with many perplexing problems.

At his headquarters in New York City, Sir Henry

Clinton was in a quandary. He did not dare risk an attack on Washington, and he had become increasingly doubtful that he would get strong support from the loyalists, who had exaggerated both their own numbers and their willingness to fight with the British troops. But the War Office in London, far removed from the American scene, clung to the hope that assistance would come from the loyal supporters of the King. According to report, they would be found in the South. There, it was said, the Tories outnumbered the patriots and were eager to take up arms against them. So the fateful decision to invade the southern states was made.

The campaign was launched in sparsely settled Georgia. In December 1778 Savannah fell, and a month later Augusta. With all of Georgia under British control, and with the departure of the French fleet for the West Indies after several failures, Clinton himself sailed southward with 8,000 troops to lay siege to Charleston, South Carolina. Although the city was well fortified, the enemy attack by land and by sea forced its surrender in May 1780. It was a shattering blow to the patriots, and a jubilant Clinton was confident that he would soon have control of the eastern seaboard from Georgia to New York. He returned north, leaving Lord Cornwallis in command in the South.

As Cornwallis began to drive northward, the patriots of both Georgia and South Carolina suddenly turned to guerrilla warfare with the fury of hornets that had been poked out of their nests. The southern terrain with its rivers and swamps and forests was ideal for their swift and punishing attacks under the leadership of the brilliant and courageous Francis Marion—the "Swamp Fox"—Thomas Sumter, Andrew Pickens, and others. Washington and the Congress were also sending down more Continentals and reinforcements of artillery, and in that summer of 1780 a French squadron and a French army of 6,000 men under Comte de Rochambeau arrived at Newport, Rhode Island.

Nonetheless, Cornwallis scored a smashing victory at Camden, South Carolina. But in North Carolina, where Tory support fell far short of what he expected, the patriots struck back successfully at Kings Mountain and at the Cowpens in January 1781. Two months later the British General won another victory at Guilford Court House in North Carolina.

But Cornwallis, so unlike Sir William Howe in his boldness and aggressive drive, had exhausted his army and destroyed all his heavy baggage in order to move faster. Because the interior of North Carolina was not safe under these conditions, he marched off to Virginia in the spring of 1781.

And now the Americans and the French cooperated in a bold move to trap Cornwallis at Yorktown, Virginia, where he had holed up. Lafayette, already with the patriot troops in nearby Williamsburg, was warned not to let the British General escape. With Admiral de Grasse's assurance that he would be in the Chesapeake with his fleet of twenty-eight vessels and a force of French regulars by September, Washington and Rochambeau hurried south with the bulk of the Franco-American army. The plan was carried out with smooth efficiency and masterly execution. Finding himself surrounded by a superior army and the Chesapeake blocked by the enemy fleet, Lord Cornwallis surrendered all his forces on October 19, 1781.

Although a formal peace treaty would not be signed until almost two years later, Cornwallis' surrender at Yorktown brought the long war to an end. For the victorious patriots, independence had been won. For stubborn and foolish King George, the "black tidings" of Yorktown marked the end of his control over the American colonies—no longer colonies now, but the free and independent states of America.

In the summer of 1781, while the Revolution moved rapidly toward its momentous climax, the authorities in Philadelphia took long-delayed action in ordering the removal of the decayed wooden steeple above the brick tower of the State House. Edmund Woolley was no longer there to supervise the work. The carpenter now responsible for the alterations was Thomas Nevell, who was assisted by

John Coburn, a rigger employed by Nevell in "getting down the old steeple and getting up the Bell and fixing of it." With its steeple gone—and another would not be built for almost fifty years—the grace and beauty of the State House were diminished. Thomas Nevell covered the brick tower with a low, sloping hip roof surmounted by a slender finial.

Unfortunately, the Bell began to slip into obscurity at this time, from which it would not emerge for many years. There are fragmentary records of its having rung on a few occasions during the next half-century, but no records have yet been found of other times when it probably did ring. A few years after it was taken down into the tower by Nevell and his rigger, the committee of the Assembly responsible for repairs to the State House reported on "hanging the Bell in the upper brick story, and setting three of the windows with sounding boards." This item makes it fairly certain that the Bell *was* rung while hanging in an upper story of the tower.

The Congress was now back in session at the State House, and on October 24 Washington's aide, Lieutenant Colonel Tench Tilghman, brought the "Victory Dispatch" and the full story of Cornwallis's defeat to the excited and exultant delegates. There followed a frenzy of celebration in the city. Cheering crowds thronged the streets and attended services of thanksgiving in the churches. Cannon boomed from ships in the harbor, artillery roared in the State House Yard, and the bells pealed joyously. It is not likely that the Bell was silent. The doorkeeper of the Assembly must have climbed the stairs to its tower room and set the great clapper to clanging—to proclaiming the liberty that been won by all the brave patriots, many of whom had given their lives in the cause of freedom.

After a brief rest at Mount Vernon on the Potomac, the Commander in Chief came to Philadelphia in November accompanied by Mrs. Washington. During a stay of nearly four months, they occupied Benjamin Chew's new house on South Third Street. Washington conferred often with the Congress and spent long hours at his desk writing letters and reports. On the last day of March 1782, he returned to his troops at Newburgh, New York.

At last, on April 19, 1783, exactly eight years after Lexington and Concord, the "cessation of hostilities between the United States of America and the King of Great Britain" was formally announced to the army. On the following fourth of December, Washington bade farewell to his officers at noon in New York's Fraunces Tavern. Lifting a glass of wine, he said feelingly: "With a heart full of love and gratitude, I now take leave of you. I most devoutly wish that your latter days may be as prosperous and happy as your former ones have been glorious and honorable."

Benjamin Franklin had stayed on in Paris after having been appointed to the American peace commission. After the British had signed a provisional treaty in November 1782, he wrote to the Congress saying: "I am now entering my seventy-eighth year; public business has engrossed fifty of them; I wish now to be, for the little time I have left, my own master. If I live to see this peace concluded, I shall beg leave to remind the Congress of their promise then to dismiss me. I shall be happy to sing with Old Simeon: 'Now lettest thy servant depart in peace, for mine eyes have seen salvation.' "

Franklin did live to see the peace concluded when, on September 3, 1783, the formal treaties between America and France and England were signed. But it was not until two years later that the Congress let its old servant depart in peace. In May 1785, he returned to Philadelphia and to such a welcome as no other citizen of the Quaker City had ever been given. The festivities and the ceremonies lasted a week, which would have worn out anyone except the venerable sage, who took it all calmly and then accepted a seat on the state's supreme Executive Council.

Since his duties would be light, Franklin settled down happily to enlarging his home on Market Street and to making himself comfortable in his library. He devised a fan that he worked with his foot, a chair that opened into a stepladder, and a mechanical hand that could lift down books from the upper shelves.

While Franklin puttered with his inventions and supervised the alterations on his house, preparations were in progress down on Chestnut Street for the approaching Federal Constitutional Convention. Workmen were busy making extensive repairs and improvements on both the interior and the exterior of the State House. Gardeners were at work in the Yard, too, providing "more walks, shaded with trees, a pleasant lawn, and several beds of shrubs and flowers."

In 1783 there had been a disturbance at the State House when it was surrounded by a body of mutinous soldiers demanding back pay from the Congress. Its members were not harmed, but the incident led to their moving to Princeton, and they never returned to the State House.

The Continental Congress, which would soon come to an end, had served the young nation ably. During the war years, when it had dealt with so many complex problems, it had also worked out a plan of government that had been adopted by the thirteen states. Recognizing the need now for a stronger government than could be effected by the Articles of Confederation, the Congress called a convention "to form a more perfect Union."

Delegates to the Federal Constitutional Convention assembled in Philadelphia on May 25, 1787.

And once more the Assembly Room in the State House became the setting for a historic event. Here where the Declaration of Independence had been adopted, able men now sat to frame a constitution for the United States. There were fifty-five delegates, most of whom had served in the Congress or in high office in their own states. Eight had signed the Declaration of Independence. Washington was again a member of a notable delegation from Virginia, and he was named chairman of the Convention by unanimous vote.

And Benjamin Franklin, the patriarch and seer, had left the carpet-slippered comfort of his library to serve his country yet once more, and for the last time. He headed Pennsylvania's delegation, and although past eighty, he was mentally alert. His role in the Convention was confined mainly to advising younger members and acting as peacemaker. But that was not all. At the close of the Convention on September 17, the old philosopher made his own unique observation that has been remembered and recounted long after the oratory of those four months had been forgotten.

While arguments waxed heatedly and controversies swirled around him, Franklin gazed reflectively at the carved design of half the sun that ornamented the top of the high-back chair in which Washington sat on a raised platform. Since the representation of the rising and the setting sun was the same, he said, and with the outcome of the Convention at times so uncertain, he could not decide which would be the appropriate symbol. But now that the work was completed, he added, he had no doubt that it was a rising, not a setting, sun that should symbolize the signing of the Constitution.

There had been no argument about who should serve the new nation as its first President. By common consent, this honor was conferred upon George Washington. When the Constitution was finally ratified by all the states, it was decided that the new government should begin operation on March 4, 1789, and that for the first year New York City should be the capital. The Residence Act stipulated that for the next ten years Philadelphia should be the seat of government. Afterward, the permanent capital was to be situated on the Potomac River.

Shortly before the Federal Government moved from New York to Philadelphia, two new buildings were completed on the State House Square—the City Hall on the east and the County Courthouse on the west side of the State House. Both buildings conformed in style to the others on the Square. Then, in 1790, with the change in the seat of the government, the United States Supreme Court was given the use of the new City Hall (now known as the Supreme Court Building), and Congress was offered the new County Courthouse (now known as Congress Hall). The House of Representatives sat in the large room on the first floor of Congress Hall, and the United States Senate met in a room on the second floor.

Provision for the President's house was made by Robert Morris, close friend of Washington and a wealthy merchant and banker who had helped finance the Revolution. The Morris town house that President and Mrs. Washington occupied for the rest of his years as Chief Executive was a three-story mansion on the south side of High Street west of Fifth.

Here the President held a formal reception every second Tuesday between three and four in the afternoon. He wore a black velvet suit, with powdered hair gathered behind in a silk snood, and held in his gloved hand a cocked hat with a black cockade in it. Riding in his cream-colored coach drawn by six long-tailed Virginia bays, or strolling the streets with no fear of lowering his dignity, President Washington became a familiar figure to the citizens of Philadelphia in that last decade of the eighteenth century.

On March 4, 1793, George Washington was inaugurated for his second term in the Senate Chamber on the second floor of Congress Hall. Before retiring, he delivered his last formal message to Congress in the Chamber of the House of Representatives downstairs on December 7, 1796. And here in the lower Chamber, two years after John Adams became the second President of the United States on March 4,

1797, official news of Washington's death at Mount Vernon was received by Congress.

In that December of 1799, General Henry (Light-Horse Harry) Lee delivered a funeral oration in Philadelphia's Old Zion Lutheran Church in which he spoke the words that became the immortal Washington's epitaph: "First in war, first in peace, first in the hearts of his countrymen."

IX

The Cracked Bell

FOR PENN'S fair city on the Delaware, the high tide of history receded at the close of the eighteenth century. The Federal Government moved to Washington, and the State Government to Lancaster, Pennsylvania. At the beginning of the new century, Philadelphia ceased to be a capital city. And for the first time since the Assembly moved into its east room back in 1735, the State House stood empty. Suddenly, where the voices of great men had resounded in debate on momentous issues, there was silence.

Then, in 1802, a distinguished citizen of Philadelphia was given permission to use the second floor of the State House as a museum of natural history and portrait gallery. Charles Willson Peale, who had fought as a Continental soldier at Trenton and Germantown, was an exceptionally versatile man—an American portrait painter of distinction, an engraver, and a naturalist. He had painted the portraits of many of the famous men of the times, including more than a dozen of George Washington.

Peale moved his stuffed birds from Philosophical Hall to the long room on the second floor of the State House and arranged them neatly in partitioned recesses on one wall. The stuffed animals occupied the opposite side of the room where the naturalist's prize exhibit stood—the skeletons of two mastodons that he himself had excavated at a site in New York. The portraits were hung on the east and west walls of the room.

It had been agreed that Peale would be responsible for the maintenance of both the building and the Yard. And the State House was fortunate in having had him as a tenant, for he took excellent care of it, and improved the appearance of the Yard by planting more trees and adding new gates and benches.

But this was a dark period for the historic old building—so dark that it came perilously close to being demolished. On the thirteenth of March 1815, the Governor of Pennsylvania signed an act that authorized the county commissioners of Philadelphia to take charge of the State House and rent as much of its space as they could. One year later, the legislators took even more drastic and appalling steps to raise money for building the new capitol at Harrisburg.

They passed a bill that provided for the appointment of three commissioners who would have the Square divided into lots that would be put up for sale for a minimum total of $150,000. There was a provision, however, that gave Philadelphia the privilege of purchasing the Square with its buildings for $70,000. And it became the good fortune of all Americans that the city officials promptly bought the property and took title to it in March 1818.

The city commissioners had shown little concern, though, in preserving the old buildings as they were. Some years before their purchase from the state, they had been granted authority to make changes. They tore down the old wings and replaced them with two row buildings attached to the east and west ends of the State House. These ugly structures were used mainly for storing records. Then the Assembly Room was "modernized" for use as a courtroom by the removal of its paneling, for which plaster and paint were substituted. Nor was that all. As if bent on destroying everything that was beautiful, the commissioners had the simple colonial doorway to the State House from Chestnut Street taken down and an ornate one put up in its place.

When it seemed that the citizens of Philadelphia were rapidly forgetting their historic past, the visit of a celebrated and beloved foreigner jolted them out of their apathy. The year was 1824, and with news that the Marquis de Lafayette was coming to the city late in September, interest in the old State House as a shrine was suddenly awakened. Of course elaborate preparations should be made for the visit of the noble Frenchman who had come to America as a young man to fight with Washington for the cause of American freedom. And what better place to pay him homage than the old State House where the Declaration of Independence had been adopted and the Constitution had been framed?

The architect William Strickland designed a huge arch, its framework covered with canvas painted to look like stone, that was erected across Chestnut Street in front of the State House. Now they were calling the Assembly Room the Hall of Independence, and whatever occupant it had at the time was chased out and the room "fitted up in the most splendid manner."

The windows were hung with red and blue draperies studded with stars. In the recess between the fireplaces along the east wall a statue of Washington was placed, flanked on the right by portraits of Penn and Franklin, and on the left by those of Robert Morris and Francis Hopkinson. A Peale portrait of Washington, draped in red and blue folds suspended from spears and laurel wreaths, hung over the entrance door, and on the west wall were more portraits—of Jefferson, Hancock, Adams, Madison, Monroe, and Charles Thomson.

Lafayette was welcomed by cheering throngs when he arrived in the city on September 28. He was driven in an open barouche drawn by four white horses in a long procession that moved slowly toward the State House, with the band playing martial music and the bells pealing. As the barouche passed through the curved opening in the great arch, with the wooden figures of Justice and Wisdom standing rigidly to the right and the left in their niches, the distinguished Frenchman may have heard the measured clanging of a bell different from all the rest. For surely the Bell was rung to greet him.

The aging Lafayette, now approaching seventy, was formally received in the Hall of Independence by the Mayor and other dignitaries. And here among the portraits of notable Americans he knew, or had known, he was the honored guest at levees, or receptions, during his week-long visit. Members of the clergy, of the American Philosophical Society, and of the bar association came to pay their respects and to address him in words of praise. The schoolchildren came, too, troops of them, to stare in wide-eyed wonder at the old Frenchman who was a hero of America's Revolution.

After the memorable reception Philadelphia gave the Marquis, there were no more big public celebrations until the Fourth of July 1826. On that day the oratory and the cannon's boom reverberated across the land as every city, town, and hamlet celebrated the Fiftieth Anniversary of the Declaration of Independence. In the Quaker City, festive with banners and flags, there were parades "both numerous and splendid." On the Common and in the harbor the big guns fired salvos, and the multitude that gathered in the State House Yard, under the blazing July sun, listened to orations and to a reading of the famous Declaration that had been read for the first time there by Colonel John Nixon on the eighth of July 1776. But the real drama of this Fiftieth Anniversary took place elsewhere—in two widely separated places.

In his beautiful white-domed mansion, Thomas Jefferson lay dying when the first reports of cannon fired in Charlottesville, Virginia, three miles to the west, rolled up to Monticello. He was now eighty-three, and years earlier he had built his lovely home brick by brick here on the "little mountain." Around it lay the fields and orchards he loved, bright green and gold in the shimmering July heat. And far beyond, the Blue Ridge rose mistily along the western horizon.

The man who at thirty-three had written the Declaration of Independence, and who had been America's third President, lay propped up in bed, conscious but slowly sinking. As the sound of the booming cannon came through the open windows, the doctor leaned over the long, gaunt figure and gently said, "You have lived to see the Fourth of July and the Fiftieth Anniversary of the day you have rendered glorious." A few hours later Thomas Jefferson was dead.

On that same Fourth of July in sleepy little Quincy, Massachusetts, ninety-one-year-old John Adams, America's second President, had feebly asked to be moved into his study where it was cooler. Here in the big white clapboard-and-brick house, shaded by chestnuts and elms, he too heard for the last time the salutes fired in honor of Independence Day, for which he had worked so hard. He and his good friend Thomas Jefferson had served their country for over half a century, and theirs had been a warm friendship for almost as long. At sundown John Adams murmured his last words: "Thomas Jefferson survives." He died not knowing that he had outlived his old friend by a few hours.

Interest in the State House that Lafayette's visit had stimulated did not pass with the departure from Philadelphia of the famous visitor. It was as if the city had rediscovered the historic old building, and had realized for the first time what a precious heritage it represented. Veneration for it as a shrine, and concern for its preservation, began then and have continued into the present.

At last, in the summer of 1828, a wooden steeple, to replace the one that had been removed in 1781, was built on top of the tower. Designed by William Strickland, it was a restoration rather than an exact replica of the earlier one. The main deviations from the original were the installation of a clock in the new steeple and the use of more ornamental detail. Funds were also provided for the purchase of a larger bell to be cast by John Wilbank, and Isaiah Lukens was commissioned to make the clock.

Two years later, the city fathers responded to public interest by taking steps to have the Assembly Room, or Hall of Independence, restored "to its ancient form." A citizen visiting the building in October 1831 reported that he found the room "undergoing repairs in order to render the appearance similar to that which it bore when our ancestors there assembled on the 4th of July 1776." But there was no longer any need, or ever would be, to use the old room as it had been used when "our ancestors" gathered there during the stirring times of the Revolutionary period.

Uncertain of what use to make of it, and recalling Lafayette's reception there, members of the City Councils finally decided it should serve as a levee room for distinguished visitors to the city. So the Assembly Room now entered what could be called its levee period. On June 10, 1833, President Andrew Jackson received the citizens of Philadelphia here, and during the next quarter-century levees were held by many other presidents of the United States, and by the great and the famous in various fields.

The old Bell, hanging in an upper story of the tower, was not disturbed while the work of reconstruction and restoration went on elsewhere. Its voice had not yet been silenced, but like those great "ancestors" who had walked off the stage for the last time, the Bell was nearing the end of its useful life.

One by one, the makers and movers of the early history of the young nation had gone. Benjamin Franklin, first citizen of Philadelphia and citizen of the world, had died in April 1790; John Hancock, wealthy Boston patriot and able president of the Continental Congress, in October 1793; Richard Henry Lee, the Virginia orator who had proposed the resolution for declaring independence, in June 1794; and Sam Adams, the great agitator for independence, in October 1803. With the death of Charles Carroll in November 1832, no living signer of the Declaration of Independence was left. And two years later, in May 1834, Lafayette died in Paris.

The last of those first towering figures who had been prominent in shaping the destiny of their country was the distinguished American jurist John Marshall. He was Chief Justice of the Supreme Court of the United States when he died in Philadelphia on July 6, 1835. According to tradition, the muffled Bell tolled slowly two days later as his body was borne through the streets of the city to the steamboat that carried him back to his native Virginia for burial. And also according to tradition, it was while tolling for the "great Chief Justice" that the Bell cracked.

How often, and when, the Bell had rung in those later years is not known. But there is evidence that it did ring on occasion. One of the few newspaper references to it appeared in the *Public Ledger* on February 26, 1846. In that issue it was reported that "the old Independence Bell rang its last clear note on Monday last (February 22) in honor of the birthday of Washington, and now hangs in the tower irreparably cracked and dumb." The crack had appeared before, it was stated, but repairs had been attempted by filing the edges of the fractures so there would be no vibration, one against the other. The Bell had rung out, clear and loud, and had seemed to be in good condition. But at noon it shuddered into silence when it received "a sort of compound fracture in a zigzag direction through one side."

There was the metallurgist who explained that when metal of the Bell's composition is remelted several times it loses bending quality and becomes brittle like glass. But the old Bell, after three castings, had for all its brittleness lasted a long time. It had fulfilled its prophecy of proclaiming "liberty throughout all the land unto all the inhabitants thereof." Then, with dramatic fitness, it had become mute at the end of the era that had created the United States and had laid the foundation for its perpetuation.

X

Symbolism of the Bell

IT IS a puzzling fact that for some time prior to the summer of 1851, the City Councils had permitted the cellar of the old State House to be used as a dog pound. It is unexplained, too, why they resolved on July 3 "that the cellar of Independence Hall shall not, from this time forth, be used as a receptacle for dogs taken up under the Ordinances." The yelping strays may have been turned out because of complaints about the noise they made. Or the Council members may have come to feel some embarrassment about putting even the cellar of the historic old building to such undignified use—and especially since there would be an important meeting held there the following summer.

For in the fall of that year of 1851, each of the thirteen original states was requested to appoint delegates to a convention in Independence Hall on July 4, 1852. The purpose of the gathering was to discuss plans for erecting suitable monuments in the Square to commemorate the Declaration of Independence. Though nothing was accomplished at this convention, in preparation for it the old Bell was at last noticed, and was brought down for public display in the Assembly Room.

Even the newspapers took note of this long-delayed recognition. On July 2, 1852, the Philadelphia *Inquirer* reported: "The Committee on city property have caused the old Independence Bell to be lowered from its elevation in the State House tower, and placed in the Hall of Independence on an octagon pedestal, covered with green baize, where it will remain hereafter."

At this time the Assembly Room was sparsely furnished with a few paintings and a wooden statue of Washington, carved by William Rush, which stood in the recess in the center of the east wall. Charles Willson Peale had died in 1827, and his museum had been removed from Independence Hall. When his oil portraits were put up for sale in 1854, the city purchased more than a hundred of them. Some of these paintings were then hung in the Assembly Room, and more furniture was brought in.

As if to compensate for long years of neglect, the Bell was given an elaborate new pedestal, which was placed in the southeast corner of the room. The thirteen sides, representing the thirteen original states, were festooned with flags and ornamented with Roman fasces, liberty caps, and the names of the signers of the Declaration. And perched on top of the Bell, with outspread wings, was Charles Willson Peale's fierce-looking stuffed eagle.

On Washington's birthday in 1855, the Assembly Room was formally opened to the public by the Mayor. And during the next few years prior to the outbreak of the Civil War, an ever-increasing number of visitors came to the Hall of Independence—both the famous and the ordinary people from all walks of life.

It was Washington's birthday again in 1861 when a tall, lanky, rawboned man who had been a humble rail-splitter honored both the nation's first President and the old State House. On that February 22, President-elect Abraham Lincoln presided in a ceremony at which he raised the flag of the United States in front of Independence Hall on Chestnut Street.

What he said on that occasion is not so well known as his more famous utterances are, notably the Gettysburg Address. But even the brief remarks he made that day are memorable for depth of feeling, simple eloquence, and profound awareness of the significance of the Declaration of Independence and the place of its origin. Lincoln said:

> I am filled with deep emotion at finding myself standing in this place, where were collected together the wisdom, the patriotism, the devotion to principle, from which sprang the institutions under which we live. You have kindly suggested to me that in my hands is the task of restoring peace to the present distracted condition of the country. I can say in return, Sir, that all the political sentiments I entertain have been drawn, so far as I have been able to draw them, from the sentiments which originated and were given to the world from this hall. I have never had a feeling politically that did not spring from the sentiments embodied in the Declaration of Independence.

The flag that Abraham Lincoln raised in front of Independence Hall, which had been the setting for the birth of the nation, did not wave long over the United States of America. Less than two months later, those states were sundered by the war that began on April 12, 1861. Lincoln had gone on to the White House in Washington to carry the terrible burdens of the war years, determined to preserve the Union at any cost. What it cost him in grief came to be deeply etched in his craggy face and reflected in the brooding sadness of his deep-set eyes. On New Year's Day in 1863, he became the "great Emancipator" when he signed the Emancipation Proclamation that freed the Negro slaves.

Now and again during these years of bloody strife, a reception was held in the Declaration Chamber for a distinguished officer of the Union Army, but more often the bodies of the slain lay in state here. And on the twenty-second of April 1865, a grieving multitude came to pay their last respects to the Commander in Chief himself.

Abraham Lincoln had been elected to his second term as President, and in his second inaugural address he had spoken the memorable phrase: "With malice toward none; with charity for all." The South would be welcomed back into the Union, not crushed by the heel of the conqueror. Lincoln lived to see the end of the war on April 9, 1865, but on the night of the fourteenth, when attending a performance at Ford's Theater, he was shot by the mad actor John Wilkes Booth, and died the next morning.

The martyred President's funeral journey, which took him back to his home in Springfield, Illinois, included most of the stops he had made four years and two months before on the way to his first inaugural. In Philadelphia, at noon on Saturday, April 22, a half-million people met the funeral train. Everywhere, black crape and black bunting bespoke the city's grief. When the black-draped casket was placed in the Declaration Chamber, there soon formed a line of patient mourners that extended back for three miles. And like a guard of honor for the silent dead, the mute Bell stood above the still form in the open coffin.

For three decades before the Civil War, there had been agitation in the North against the institution of slavery. Those who crusaded for the emancipation of the Negro slaves were called abolitionists, and it was in connection with this movement that the Bell was first deliberately used as a symbol of freedom.

Sometime in the year of 1839, an unknown person—quite likely an abolitionist—noticed the Bell's inscription. It is certain that he discussed it with other freedom crusaders, for in that same year an antislavery pamphlet entitled *The Liberty Bell* was published. Thus, as far as is known, the Bell was given the name by which it has become famous. Previously, it had occasionally been called the Old State House Bell, the Bell of the Revolution, or Old Independence Bell. It remained for those who crusaded for the freedom of the slaves to give it the perfect name. Other publications followed that carried idealized pictures of the Bell, but its use as a symbol of freedom was limited to efforts to abolish slavery.

Now that the Bell had been rescued from obscurity and publicized, its evolution as a patriotic symbol and a revered relic was the next logical step. The man who did more than any other to bring this about was not anonymous. His name was George Lippard, a popular novelist of Philadelphia who wrote a vividly fanciful tale about the Bell that aroused patriotic enthusiasm and became very popular. The title of the story was "Fourth of July, 1776," one of a collection called *Legends of the Revolution,* which first appeared in 1847 in the Philadelphia *Saturday Courier.*

As Lippard told the story, the Fourth of July 1776 was a cloudless summer day. Crowds had gathered along Chestnut Street in front of the State House, and among little groups on the back lawn were the merchant, the mechanic, the bearded sailor, the dark-robed minister. There was an expression of anxiety on every face.

Up in the wooden steeple, a white-haired old man with sunburned face was trying to read the inscription on the Bell that hung suspended there. Finally he gave up, and turned to a flaxen-haired boy who stood beside him. He was a rich man's son, this lad with laughing eyes of summer blue, so of course he could read. Would he spell out the words for the old man, who was no scholar?

The boy quickly raised himself on tiptoe, and, grasping the rim of the Bell, read aloud: "PROCLAIM LIBERTY THROUGHOUT ALL THE LAND UNTO ALL THE INHABITANTS THEREOF."

The old man thought about the strange words for

a few moments. Then he urged the boy to hurry downstairs and to wait in the hall by a big door until a man should come out and give him a word. Whereupon, he must run out into the street and shout it up to the old bell-keeper. The boy turned and sped to do his bidding, hastening down the dark stairs on nimble feet.

Alone in the steeple, the old man waited impatiently. Time passed, and he leaned over the railing facing Chestnut Street, looking anxiously for sight of the fair-haired boy. Perhaps he had forgotten. But as the old bell-keeper was thinking of having to totter down and up the stairs again on his shaky old legs, he heard a merry laugh. Ah, there he was, standing on tiptoe with his fair hair blown about his face, and up came the single shouted word: *"Ring!"*

Withered hands grasped the iron tongue of the Bell. The old man felt young again. Backward and forward he swung the clapper with sturdy strokes. Again and again he hurled it while sweat poured from his brow. *Boom! Boom! Boom!* The Bell spoke to the city and the world. The sound crossed the Atlantic, pierced the dungeons of Europe, the workshops of England, the vassal-fields of France.

Why did the State House Bell speak such deep and awful meaning to the world?

Because in an old hall, down under the Bell, fifty-six traders, farmers, and mechanics had signed a Parchment that was brought in by the Committee of

Three—by Thomas Jefferson, John Adams, and Benjamin Franklin. And those fifty-six signatures had shaken off the shackles of the world.

Certainly the people of Philadelphia knew that Lippard's story of what happened on the Fourth of July 1776 was entirely his own invention, a figment of his imagination. Hence, the authenticity given it by the historian Benson J. Lossing is puzzling.

Lossing achieved some fame and standing as a historian by writing a bulky volume entitled *The Pictorial Field Book of the Revolution.* To gather material for it at firsthand, he left New York on November 22, 1848, on a journey that took him to the "southern portions of the old Thirteen States." He traveled in his own conveyance, "a light dearborn wagon drawn by a strong, good-natured horse." Arriving in Philadelphia a few days later, Lossing explored the city's landmarks, particularly the old State House. When he came to write his book, he recorded Lippard's Fourth of July story without questioning its historical accuracy.

The readers who became familiar with Lippard's fictional tale (and believed it) multiplied after Benson Lossing's book appeared, for it too was widely read. A few years later, the story had an even wider circulation when another minor, but popular, historian made use of it. Joel Tyler Headley included it, with variations, in his *Life of George Washington,* which was first published serially in 1854 in

Graham's Magazine. The cover of the magazine for the June issue of that year pictured the old bell-keeper, with tight little pigtail stiffly erect, standing beside the Bell as the flaxen-haired boy excitedly mounts the platform.

Other popular historians had a part in spreading the legend, and then the writers of patriotic verse appropriated the exciting material. Neither the date nor the author of the first and most popular of the poems is known. With the title "Independence Bell —July 4, 1776," it had turned up in collections of patriotic verse before 1871, but in that year it found its largest number of readers when George S. Hillard gave it to the schoolchildren in his *Franklin Fifth Reader.* For years thereafter, what they knew about the first Fourth of July they learned from reading the poem "Independence Bell." There were countless recitations of it, and of the nine stanzas, these became the best known:

> There was tumult in the city,
>   In the quaint old Quaker town,
> And the streets were rife with people
>   Pacing restless up and down—
> People gathering at the corners,
>   Where they whispered each to each,
> And the sweat stood on their temples
>   With the earnestness of speech.

Hushed the people's swelling murmur,
    Whilst the boy cries joyously;
"Ring!" he's shouting, "Ring, grandfather,
    Ring! Oh, ring for Liberty!"
Quickly at the given signal
    The old Bellman lifts his hand.
Forth he sends the good news, making
    Iron music through the land.

Perhaps there is no other instance of such distortion of historical facts having so happy an outcome. It is possible, even likely, that the old Bell would have been saved from oblivion in some other way if its inscription had not first attracted the attention of the abolitionists, and later aroused the interest of the popular historians. But the facts are that it owes its resurrection to those who worked to abolish slavery, and its evolution into a patriotic relic to George Lippard and the historians who recorded his legend as historical fact.

It should be remembered, too, that the Liberty Bell owes its unique distinction to Isaac Norris, and the two other Quaker superintendents of the old State House, who were its architects. Their inspired choice of an inscription has given the Bell the preeminent place it holds among bells and in the hearts of the American people.

With the great Bell hanging aloft in the State House steeple, Isaac Norris may have reflected upon how much more it could symbolize than the religious liberty granted the people of Pennsylvania by William Penn's Charter. He may even have thought of the enslaved Negroes in the colonies who had no liberties at all, for the Quakers were the first persons in America to condemn slavery as evil, and it was the Pennsylvania Quakers who were the first to take action in a humanitarian approach to the institution of slavery.

As early as 1696, they urged their members to speak out against the slave trade, and in 1776, the year of the Declaration of Independence, all slaveholders who would not emancipate their slaves were barred from membership in the Society of Friends. Subsequently, Quakers in all the other colonies followed Pennsylvania's lead.

It was, therefore, a historic coincidence of significant interest that the Bell was lifted from dusty neglect by someone concerned about the Negroes' plight, and, of even greater interest, was given its enduring name in an antislavery pamphlet that for the first time used it as a symbol of freedom—of freedom for the slaves.

But the abolitionist, and antislavery, movement had gained momentum long before that year of 1839. George Washington had said that it was among his first wishes "to see some plan adopted by which slavery might be abolished in America by law." John Adams and Thomas Jefferson, among other distinguished Americans, had expressed their abhorrence of the practice of slaveholding.

Influenced by Benjamin Lundy, a Quaker abolitionist, William Lloyd Garrison organized the American Anti-Slavery Society in 1833, and wrote with such fanatical fervor against slavery in his publication the *Liberator* that his life was often in danger. Elijah Lovejoy paid with his life on the night of November 7, 1837, while defending his right to publish editorials condemning slavery and urging gradual emancipation. And hundreds of anonymous white sympathizers assisted Negro slaves to escape to freedom in Canada by way of the Underground Railroad—"Let the North Star be your guide," they said to the runaway slaves at parting.

Among the poets who participated in the emancipation struggle by speaking on this theme in verse, none was so dedicated to the cause of the Negro's freedom as John Greenleaf Whittier, the Quaker poet. But the most powerful appeal for sympathy in behalf of the slaves was made by Mrs. Harriet Beecher Stowe in her novel *Uncle Tom's Cabin.* Published in book form in 1852, its success was immediate and sensational. And the many translations that followed "bound the world together in a common revulsion against slavery." It was reported that President Lincoln said to Mrs. Stowe upon meeting her the first time, "So you are the little woman who wrote the book that made this great war."

No other section of the country had so large a slave population as the agricultural South. Here were the broad fields in which the unskilled African could labor, and here was the mild climate to which he could adapt. But even in the South, prior to the late eighteenth century, there was a strong feeling against the institution of slavery. Most thoughtful Southerners believed as Jefferson did that "all men are by nature free and independent," and that slavery was an evil which should be abolished.

Then, in 1793, Eli Whitney, a young inventor from New England, changed this humane conception of slavery and riveted it upon the South by his invention of the cotton gin. A tremendous increase in cotton production followed, and with a ready market in England for his product, the southern planter became wealthy, but he had to depend upon slave labor. In defense of its cotton plantations and the institution of slavery, the only recourse left the South was secession. It was this act that plunged the country into the Civil War that seemingly could not have been averted.

The Emancipation Proclamation that President Lincoln signed on January 1, 1863, freed the Negro from the bondage of slavery. But for the next hundred years he lived as a free man without the political, the economic, or the social rights of a first-class citizen. Today, led by outstanding members of his own race, he is engaged in a monumental struggle for rights long overdue.

Instead of abolitionist and antislavery crusades led by white men, there now exists the civil-rights movement with its able and articulate Negro leaders—among them, one who works for peace and brotherhood by nonviolent methods, and upon whom the Nobel Peace Prize for 1964 was bestowed. Speaking before royalty and a distinguished audience in Oslo, Norway, the Reverend Dr. Martin Luther King said that he accepted the award on behalf of "a civil-rights movement which is moving with determination and a majestic scorn for risk and danger to establish a reign of freedom and a rule of justice."

Today's unrelenting struggle for a larger share in liberty on the part of the Negro and other minority groups is as relevant to the meaning of the Liberty Bell in Independence Hall as was religious freedom for the colonists in Pennsylvania, independence for the American colonies, and emancipation for the American slaves. Gazing at the old cracked Bell, the thoughtful American will recognize this. He will understand, too, that the Liberty Bell is a symbol not only of political liberty but also of economic and social liberty, and he will ponder with fresh vision the Liberty Bell's ancient inscription:

PROCLAIM LIBERTY THROUGHOUT ALL THE LAND UNTO ALL THE INHABITANTS THEREOF. LEV. XXV. 10.

Epilogue

HAVING at last become the most venerated of patriotic shrines, Independence Hall was never again neglected. Each year it was the mecca to which more and more visitors came. Restoration followed restoration, and the meticulous work of research and reconstruction goes on today. In the years after the Civil War, the Common and Select Councils were ably assisted by the Mayor. The Philadelphia Chapter of the Daughters of the American Revolution became interested, and rendered invaluable service in behalf of the old buildings on Independence Square. And professional advice and assistance came from the American Institute of Architects early in the twentieth century.

With the approach of the Centennial of Independence in 1876, the entire first floor of Independence Hall was renovated. A 13,000-pound bell and a new clock, both of which are still in use, were given to the city at this time by Henry Seybert for the steeple of the Hall. One of the most desirable of the restoration programs was carried out between 1896 and 1898 when the ugly row buildings on each side of Independence Hall were replaced by wings and arcades closely resembling those of the eighteenth century. Finally, with the restoration of Congress Hall in 1912, and the Supreme Court Building in 1922, Independence Square was restored to the appearance of its earlier days with a group of beautifully simple and harmonious buildings.

During these years while committees and crews of workmen labored to repair the damage caused by years of neglect and careless supervision of the fine old buildings, the Liberty Bell was moved about from one place to another. At last the ideal, and permanent, arrangement for its display was made. Since 1915 it has been exhibited on a simple, sturdy frame and a low platform in the first-floor tower room just inside the south door.

The years of being moved from one place to another in Independence Hall were also the years of extensive travel, far beyond Independence Square, for the Liberty Bell. As its fame spread, requests for its appearance at expositions and special celebrations were received. The first of the Bell's many long journeys was made to New Orleans in January 1885 for exhibition at the World's Industrial and Cotton Exposition.

On that journey southward, borne on a flatcar coupled to a special train, the Bell was given the kind of joyous welcome that customarily only the President and popular heroes received. At every stop, crowds pressed forward with such eagerness to get a closer look and to touch the relic that they had to be restrained by the guards.

Among those who came to pay their respects to the Bell was one who stood out from all the rest. He was an old man, close to eighty, but still tall and erect—a proud man of dignified bearing, with clear-cut, patrician features. That man, who still dressed in suits the color of Confederate gray, was Jefferson Davis, the fallen leader of what had been the Confederate States during the Civil War—the old leader of the Lost Cause. He was passing the last years of his life in New Orleans, and he had only four more to live.

Now, with the "fierce passions of his prime cooled to the gentle wisdom of the patriarch," he stood before the Bell with his head uncovered, and said, "I believe the time has come when reason should be substituted for passion, and when we should be able to do justice to each other. Glorious old Bell, the son of a Revolutionary soldier bows in reverence before you."

For the next seven years the Bell remained in Independence Hall. Then, in April of 1893, preparations were made to take it to the World's Columbian Exposition in Chicago for display in the Pennsylvania building.

One of the most memorable of all the receptions given the old Bell was that in Allentown. Largely through the efforts of the Liberty Bell Chapter of the Daughters of the American Revolution, it was brought to Allentown on the way back to Philadelphia from Chicago.

One of the papers reported:

> The demonstration . . . was the most remarkable ever made in the Lehigh Valley. The town was a blaze of red fire when the train arrived, and every whistle shrieked out a welcome which re-echoed from the throats of thousands of people who were packed in and around the station.

Another report described the evening's gaiety:

> In honor of the old Bell's second visit, Allentown is gayer tonight than it has been for many

> a year. It is wrapped as closely as a barber's pole in red, white, and blue, and lanterns and electric lights are flashing their radiance from every building. The most conspicuous feature of the procession of 5,000 people that marched and countermarched on Hamilton Street was the passing of Zion Reformed Church where the Bell was concealed in 1777 to save it from the British, who in that year occupied Philadelphia.

There was a solemn memorial service held at the church, too. But it was not Father Blumer's old stone church under whose floor the Bell had been hidden, and which had been used as a military hospital from September 1777 to April 1778. That structure had been torn down and a third one built in 1840, and that in turn was replaced in 1888 by the present beautiful Gothic building. All four churches, however, had been erected upon the same site on Hamilton Street.

After a two-year interval, and for the last time in the nineteenth century, the Liberty Bell departed on October 3, 1895, on another journey—this time to the Cotton States and International Exposition in Atlanta, Georgia. In a little town in Virginia where the train stopped, an incident occurred that movingly brought back the Revolutionary past. Out of the usual crowd that gathered around the Bell, a white-haired old man pushed forward and asked permission to touch it. He was the great-grandson of Patrick Henry, the Virginia orator who had made a ringing plea for nationalism at the First Continental Congress.

The Bell was returned to its place in Independence Hall on February 1, 1896, where it remained undisturbed for the next six years. From January to June in 1902, it was on exhibition at the Interstate and West Indian Exposition in Charleston, South Carolina. The following year, in June 1903, it was taken to Boston for the celebration of the 128th anniversary of the Battle of Bunker Hill.

There was an especially warm place for the old Bell in the hearts of the people of Boston. The story of Philadelphia's sympathetic and generous response when Boston's port was closed was well known. Muffled, the Bell had tolled on that dark day of June 1, 1774. And it had tolled again when news of Lexington and Concord, and later of Bunker Hill, had been brought to Philadelphia.

And now, so long afterward, it was escorted through the streets of historic old Boston by the Ancient and Honorable Artillery Company. Mounted on a float festooned with flowers and drawn by thirteen horses, it occupied the place of honor in the parade that paced slowly out to the Bunker Hill Monument on Breed's Hill.

Lafayette had laid the cornerstone of the monument on June 17, 1825, on the fiftieth anniversary of the Battle of Bunker Hill. Completed in 1843, the granite shaft rose to a height of 221 feet and stood near the spot where the brave patriot Dr. Joseph Warren had fallen on the hot June day when the advancing redcoats had been repulsed again and again by the deadly fire of the outnumbered colonials. The battle scars of that day and the bloodstained salt grass were covered now by a green landscaped lawn. And the silent Bell, standing near the monument, was a fitting symbol of the liberty that had been won by sacrifice.

The following year, the City Councils of Philadelphia received a petition signed by 75,000 schoolchildren of St. Louis requesting that the Liberty Bell be sent there for display at the Louisiana Purchase Exposition. From the middle of June to the middle of November in 1904, it was again the center of attraction in the Pennsylvania State Building at a large fair. The Louisiana Exposition had links with the past, for it commemorated the centennial of the purchase, during the presidency of Thomas Jefferson, of the vast Louisiana Territory from France.

Moving on into the twentieth century, the Liberty Bell participated in a unique ceremony on February 11, 1915. On that day, transcontinental communication by telephone was successfully demonstrated. The part that the Bell played was reported by all the

Philadelphia papers, with the following account appearing in the *Public Ledger:*

> At seventeen minutes after five by Philadelphia time, and seventeen minutes after two by San Francisco time, on February 11, 1915, Mayor Blankenburg, at the office of the Bell Telephone Company, gave a signal to Chief Ball, head of the Bureau of City Property at Independence Hall, who struck the Bell with three wooden mallets. The sound of the blows was carried over the wires and was distinctly audible in San Francisco.

The echoes of those mallet strokes against the Bell had hardly faded when clamorous requests began coming in for its appearance at the Panama-Pacific Exposition in San Francisco. Again there was a petition from the schoolchildren—200,000 of them.

So the old Liberty Bell was readied on July 5, 1915, for what was to be its last journey. To the cheers of thousands and the stirring strains of "Dixie" and "The Star-Spangled Banner," it was carried, for the first time, on an automobile truck, smothered with laurel and red gladioli, to the cavernous train shed where Track 8 was reserved for the "Liberty Bell Special." A motorcade of thirty cars followed the Bell, cameras clicked along the way, and motion-picture machines whirred.

After an absence of almost five months, the Bell was brought back to Philadelphia on November 25, 1915, to its permanent place of exhibition in the tower room on the first floor of Independence Hall. Except for its appearance in a Liberty Day parade on October 25, 1917, to help sell Liberty bonds in the war effort, it has not left the Hall since then. During its travels, the crack in one side of the Bell had spread, and the decision was made after the San Francisco trip to prohibit all further travel. Now closely guarded and preserved as a priceless and irreplaceable heritage, the Liberty Bell is the chief attraction of the Quaker City.

The visitor who walks along the narrow streets and alleys of old Philadelphia feels a quickening sense of history. Unfortunately, much has been swept away. There is not a single building where Franklin worked or lived left standing. No trace remains of the old Graff house in which Jefferson wrote the Declaration of Independence. And the Robert Morris residence on Market Street west of Fifth, which Washington occupied throughout his tenure of office as President, is gone. But much of the old colonial city is still preserved in the midst of the modern metropolis.

There is one little street, a block long, on which the houses that stand on both sides are not only preserved but have been continuously lived in since colonial days. This is Elfreth's Alley, that was cut through the block between Second and Front streets just south of Race Street around the year 1700. All its quaint dwellings were built early in the eighteenth century, and three of them are among the oldest in the country. The open gutter still runs down the center of the cobblestone pavement, but fortunately it no longer serves its ancient unsanitary purpose.

These were the homes of humble people, of artisans and tailors, of riggers and dockworkers. They are typical of the many small red-brick houses that stood along Philadelphia's streets in colonial days. Each is two stories in height with a single squat dormer window projecting from the roof, and the two second-story wood-shuttered windows are topped with a heavy cornice. Several of the white brass-knockered doors have pediments, and one house has an overhang across the front above its single first-story window. A colonial lamp attached to a high pole and standing near one end of the street accents its picturesque charm.

Just a few steps south on Second Street and to the right around the corner on Arch brings one to the Betsy Ross house. Except for a roof with a steeper pitch, it is a duplicate of the little Elfreth's Alley house with the heavy overhang across the front above the first-story window. And it, too, was built early in the eighteenth century. But Betsy's skill with her needle and the story she reportedly told of having stitched together the first American flag have given her modest dwelling such fame as has come to no other little two-story red-brick house in Philadelphia. A replica of that thirteen-starred banner waves from the roof of the house that is famous as "The Birthplace of Old Glory."

The distance from the Betsy Ross house to the most historic and the most beautiful of Philadelphia's colonial churches is little more than a block. Old Christ Church with its graceful spire stands on Second Street just north of Market. Even on a sunless day, the rich interior produces an effect of radiance. On either side of the white boxed pews are stained-glass windows. An intricately wrought twenty-four-branch brass chandelier hangs from the ceiling above the center aisle. Brought over from England in 1744, it is the oldest in the country still hanging in its original place.

To the right and left, fluted white columns support arches beyond which are the sloping gallery pews with the original blue paint. This blue is repeated in the woodwork of the red-draped Palladian window back of the altar. To the left of the altar is the unique white-and-gold pulpit, shaped like a wineglass, that was designed and made in Philadelphia in 1770. The old English font was a gift sent to the church in 1697 by All Hallows Church, Barking-by-the-Tower, in London.

There is an aura of the past, too, in the historic

associations of Christ Church. The door to the southeast of the nave is that through which the first President customarily entered. And pew number fifty-eight is where President and Mrs. Washington could be seen sitting on most Sunday mornings during the years from 1790 to 1797. Farther back, Benjamin Franklin had his pew, and other members of the Continental Congress, signers of the Declaration of Independence, and other famous Americans worshiped here in Christ Church. It is still an active parish, and the ring of eight bells (later increased to eleven), cast in England and hung in the steeple in 1754, is still rung daily.

Two signers of the Declaration of Independence are buried in the churchyard, and five others, among them Benjamin Franklin, in the Burial Ground at Fifth and Arch streets. A plain stone slab covers the graves of Franklin and his wife, Deborah, in the southeast corner of the old cemetery. It is inscribed, by his instructions, with only their names and the year of his death—1790.

About ten blocks south of Christ Church, and not too long a walk on a pleasant day, is the exquisite little church that so long ago was called the cathedral in the forest. The stately old trees are gone, but Gloria Dei, with its enclosed churchyard, is an island of serenity in the busy port area of modern Philadelphia. The oldest church in Pennsylvania and the oldest in the country in continuous use, it was founded by the State Church of Sweden, and in 1845 became a member church of the Episcopal Diocese of Pennsylvania.

Here, as in Christ Church, are the white boxed pews and four smaller brass chandeliers hanging from the ceiling. But the treasured relics of the church are distinctively Swedish. Its font and the bell in the little square belfry were brought over from Gothenburg in 1642, and suspended from the ceiling are models of the ships on which the first permanent Swedish settlers came to the Delaware Valley—the *Key of Kalmar* and the *Flying Griffin.* Beneath the loft of the white-and-gold organ is a quaint religious wood carving that was also transported from Sweden in 1642. The heads of two rosy-cheeked angels are centered in widespread brown wings, and below is a representation of an open Bible with these quotations in Swedish: "The people that walked in darkness have seen a great light" (Isaiah 9:2); and "Glory to God in the highest, and on earth peace, good will toward men" (Luke 2:14).

In the churchyard are the thickly clustered white tombstones, many of them bearing ancient inscriptions. The graves are covered with ivy, and there are tall trees among them—locust, maple, poplar, and pine—that re-create the early woodland setting of the old church. In spring the air is fragrant with the delicate scent of pale pink magnolias and, later, the blossoms of the mimosa trees.

A short distance to the northwest of the Old Swedes' Church is Independence Square, and just a block east of the Square is Carpenters' Hall with its gilded weathervane above the high-domed cupola. It stands back from Fourth Street and is entered through an iron gateway supported by brick pillars. The handsome colonial building looks as fresh today as it did when, just after its completion, members of the First Continental Congress walked through its white pedimented door, and it is still used by the Carpenters' Company.

And so one comes by way of the Walnut Street entrance into what was, so many years ago, the old State House Yard. It is more like a beautiful park today, an elevation surrounded by a low brick wall with a marble coping surmounted by an iron railing. Flagstone walks, with wooden benches alongside, lead in all directions, and in summer the Square is shaded by many trees.

On October 11, 1926, the National Association of Gardeners planted thirteen red oaks here, one for each of the thirteen original states. And around the roots of each tree, soil from the state it represented was deposited. Two of these red oaks are still standing, along with many sycamores and elms, and a sprinkling of silver maples, poplars, ailanthuses, Norway maples, and one pin oak and one horse chestnut.

The four-sided gas lamps that illuminate the

Square at night were designed by Benjamin Franklin. Most of them date from 1915 when fifty-six lamps, one for each signer of the Declaration of Independence, were installed.

It is here on the south side of Independence Hall that the old tower can be seen from the first row of bricks laid by Edmund Woolley's masons to the later topmost wooden structure designed by William Strickland. Framed on either side by leafy branches during the summer, it rises sharply clear and symmetrically beautiful against the sky, the proud symbol of a people's aspirations that were realized in the old Assembly Room to the right on the ground floor of Independence Hall.

Leaving the Square to walk through the arches on the right, the visitor passes Philosophical Hall. It stands back of the Supreme Court Building (old City Hall) and is the only private building in Independence Square. It is the headquarters of the American Philosophical Society, which was founded by Franklin in 1743.

Beyond the arches and with a turn to the left, a few steps along the elm-shaded flagstone pavement brings one to the front entrance of Independence Hall, to the door through which the Founders of the Republic passed—the men of vision, courage, and hope; the men for all ages, although they wore the powdered wigs, the knee breeches, and the buckled shoes of the eighteenth century. The room in which they made their great decisions is hallowed now as the Declaration Chamber.

In this white-paneled room with the twin fireplaces and the windows to the north and the south, one feels more than a quickening sense of history. There is a quickening of the heart, too, as one recalls the scenes and the voices that enlivened the old room almost two centuries ago. John Hancock, with his hand on the gavel, sits at the President's table, as meticulous in the observance of ceremony as he is in his dress. The short, round little man who is on his feet more than anyone else and whose temper flashes like summer lightning is John Adams. There is the other Adams, too—Sam, who rarely speaks except to whisper in Cousin John's ear. The tall young man with the sensitive face and the wise old man wearing the little round spectacles are not often heard, either—but Thomas Jefferson and Benjamin Franklin are known by their deeds.

The voice that pleads for conciliation with the mother country is that of John Dickinson. And he makes his last futile plea here on the stormy afternoon of July 1, 1776. John Adams answers him with an eloquence that moves the delegates from their chairs, and the next day the fateful decision is made. Thomas Jefferson has his Declaration of Independence ready, and the United States is created here in this room on July 4, 1776, when the delegates vote for it in its final form.

It is eleven years later, and a big man of soldierly bearing sits in the President's chair. George Washington is presiding over another group of serious-minded men who sit here working through the hot summer months of 1787 on a constitution. The aged Benjamin Franklin is here again, and while the arguments fly back and forth he thoughtfully studies the wood carving of the sun on the back of Washington's chair. "I have decided that it is a rising, not a setting, sun," he is saying as the Federal Convention completes its work on the Constitution on September 17, 1787.

So Pennsylvania's old State House has become Independence Hall for the entire United States, and the Declaration of Independence has made it a shrine "honored wherever the rights of men are honored."

The Bell that rang to announce the birth of the United States, and to proclaim liberty with every stroke of the clapper, has its honored place in the small room on the ground floor of the tower. The visitor leaves the Declaration Chamber, crosses the entrance hall, and approaches the revered relic with a mixture of awe and excitement. And there it is—2,080 pounds of darkened bronze with no resonance left, but with a power to inspire reverence and affection such as no other bell has.

It hangs from the original crossbeam, a single piece of hand-hewn black walnut, with a yoke underneath cut out just enough to curve around the crown of the Bell. Spikes and bolts hold it securely to the crossbeam that is fastened on each side to an upright shaped like a wishbone. Inside, there is an iron "spider," or set of hooks, that grips the bronze shell to prevent further cracking. The wishbone supports, embossed with ornamental leaves, stand on a polished mahogany base, low enough for children to be able to reach up and touch the Bell.

Every detail of the old Liberty Bell fascinates the visitor. Its surface, both on the outside and the inside, is rough and uneven, and the lip is battered and chipped. And there is the historic crack running up from the rim in an irregular line as far as the lettering on this side. The serrated edges of the crack show the marks of the drill that was used in 1846. That was the time when it was hoped that widening the fissure would restore the Bell's sound so it could be rung to celebrate Washington's birthday, but the experiment was not successful. At the top and near the bottom of the crack, a large roundheaded bolt has been inserted to keep the parted sides from spreading, and a hairline fissure that came later extends from the upper bolt to the crown of the Bell.

More than a million people come each year to see the old Bell that had its uncertain beginnings in the iron foundry of the two humble workmen John Pass and Charles Stow, who had never before cast a bell. Having participated in the most stirring times of America's history, and having narrowly escaped destruction and oblivion, the Liberty Bell has survived to become known as a symbol of freedom throughout the world. Schoolchildren of other lands know its pictures and its replicas, and the great and the famous of many foreign countries have gazed upon it with emotion.

The happy sense of recognition upon first seeing the Bell was expressed by David Ben-Gurion, Israel's former great Premier who was born and educated in Poland. On a visit to America he was taken to Independence Hall, and at the first sight of the familiar bronze shape, he exclaimed, "Ah, the Bell!"

Today, as never before, people long oppressed are demanding freedom. Their voices can be heard in America and in many other countries. For each of them, no matter what his race or creed or color may be, the old Bell of Independence Hall proclaims liberty.

Bibliography

IN ADDITION to the source material listed below, the author is indebted to Miss Miriam Quinn, Park Historian at Independence Hall, for valuable information about the Liberty Bell and the buildings and grounds of Independence Square. Likewise, acknowledgment is made to the Reverend John C. Roak for interesting details about Gloria Dei Church, of which he is the Rector.

Adams, Charles Francis (ed.), *Works of John Adams,* Vol. II. Boston: Charles C. Little and James Brown, 1850.

Alden, John Richard. *The American Revolution, 1775–1783.* New York: Harper and Brothers, 1954.

Alexander, Mary D. *Andrew McNair and the Liberty Bell.* Chicago: The University of Chicago Press, 1929.

Allan, Herbert S. *John Hancock: Patriot in Purple.* New York: The Beechhurst Press, 1953.

American Heritage (eds.). *Let Freedom Ring: The Story of Independence Hall.* New York: American Heritage Publishing Company, 1962.

Barton, George. *Old Philadelphia.* Philadelphia: The Peter Reilly Company, 1925.

Bowen, Catherine Drinker. *John Adams and the American Revolution.* Boston: Little, Brown and Company, 1949.

Canby, Henry Seidel. *The Brandywine.* New York: Farrar and Rinehart, 1941.

Crane, Verner W. *Benjamin Franklin and a Rising People.* Boston: Little, Brown and Company, 1954.

Faris, John T. *The Romance of Old Philadelphia.* Philadelphia: J. B. Lippincott Company, 1918.

Franklin, Benjamin. *Autobiography and Selections from His Other Writings.* New York: The Modern Library, 1950.

Johnson, Gerald W. *Pattern for Liberty: The Story of Old Philadelphia.* New York: The McGraw-Hill Book Company, 1952.

Keyser, Charles S. *The Liberty Bell.* Philadelphia: Allen, Lane and Scott's Printing House, 1893.

Kraus, Michael. *The United States to 1865.* Ann Arbor: The University of Michigan Press, 1959.

Lippard, George. *Legends of the American Revolution.* Philadelphia: T. B. Peterson and Brothers, 1876.

Lossing, Benson J. *The Pictorial Field Book of the Revolution,* Vol. II. New York: Harper and Brothers, 1852.

Malone, Dumas. *Jefferson the Virginian.* Boston: Little, Brown and Company, 1948.

———. *The Story of the Declaration of Independence.* New York: Oxford University Press, 1954.

Miller, John C. *Sam Adams: Pioneer in Propaganda.* Boston: Little, Brown and Company, 1936.

Repplier, Agnes. *Philadelphia: The Place and the People.* New York: The Macmillan Company, 1898.

Riley, Edward M. *History of the Independence Hall Group.* Reprinted from *Historic Philadelphia. Transactions of the American Philosophical Society,* Vol. 43, Part I, March 1953.

Rosewater, Victor. *The Liberty Bell.* New York: D. Appleton and Company, 1926.

Sandburg, Carl. *Abraham Lincoln: The Prairie Years and the War Years.* New York: Harcourt, Brace and Company, 1954.

Scheer, George F., and Hugh F. Rankin. *Rebels and Redcoats.* New York: The World Publishing Company, 1957.

Smith, R. A. *Philadelphia as It Is.* Philadelphia: Lindsay and Blakiston, 1852.

Stoudt, John Baer. *The Liberty Bell in Allentown.* Allentown: Press of Berkemeyer, Keck and Company, 1927.

Tourtellot, Arthur B. *The Charles.* New York: Farrar and Rinehart, 1941.

Watson, John F. *Annals of Philadelphia and Pennsylvania,* Vol. I. Philadelphia: Edwin S. Stuart, 1857.

Wilson, Robert H. (ed.). *Philadelphia.* New York: C. S. Hammond and Company, 1964.

Index